Margrit Coates is an extraordinary healer who, through her love and passion for animals, now specialises exclusively as an animal healer. Her work as an animal healer and teacher is internationally acclaimed. Together with a homeopathic veterinary surgeon and a veterinary physiotherapist, Margrit is a partner in a clinic offering natural therapies for animals. She receives referrals from veterinarians who recognise the valuable role that hands-on healing plays in the well-being of animals.

Margrit's favourite way to relax when not giving healing with animals is … to be with animals, because she says she finds them very healing to be with. She also loves music and is involved in projects that combine healing energy with music especially suitable for animal healing.

By the same author:

Healing for Horses – the essential guide
to using healing energy with horses

Hands-on Healing for Pets

The Animal Lover's Essential Guide to Using Healing Energy

Margrit Coates

RIDER

LONDON · SYDNEY · AUCKLAND · JOHANNESBURG

7 9 10 8 6

First published in 2003 by Rider,
an imprint of Ebury Press, Random House,
20 Vauxhall Bridge Road, London SW1V 2SA

Random House Australia (Pty) Limited
20 Alfred Street, Milsons Point, Sydney,
New South Wales 2061, Australia

Random House New Zealand Limited
18 Poland Road, Glenfield,
Auckland 10, New Zealand

Random House (Pty) Limited
Isle of Houghton, Corner of Boundary Road & Carse O Gowrie
Houghton 2198, South Africa

Random House Publishers India Private Limited
301 World Trade Tower, Hotel Intercontinental Grand Complex,
Barakhamba Lane, New Delhi 110 001, India

The Random House Group Limited Reg. No. 954009

Papers used by Rider are natural, recyclable products made from wood grown
in sustainable forests.

Photography inside book by Jon Banfield
Pencil illustrations by Bob Ebdon
Printed and bound by Scotprint

A CIP catalogue record for this book
is available from the British Library

ISBN 9781844130511

PLEASE NOTE:

The information given in this book is intended as a self-help guide for you and
your pets. It is not to be taken as a replacement or a substitute for professional
veterinary or medical advice. Hands-on healing is a therapy to be used alongside
the care, treatment and advice provided by a veterinary surgeon, and a veterinary
surgeon must always be consulted for any concerns or problems whatsoever with a
pet or other animal. Neither the author nor the publisher can be held responsible
for any loss or claim arising out of the use or misuse of the suggestions made in
this book nor the failure to take professional veterinary advice.

I dedicate this book to every animal that needs our help.
Millions of pleas echoing in the energy of this universe.
May we hear them all.

Contents

Testimonials

'I am in favour of animal healing, my own horses have responded to Margrit's work and my horse carer is deeply into all things mysterious such as the power of healing. I have always found that healers are calm and unobtrusive people who seem to be able to pass on their calmness to a troubled animal. Certainly this was my experience with Margrit. It is most interesting to read of her encounters with different creatures and the beautiful thing about it is that there are no harmful substances or side-effects with this kind of medicine.'

Carla Lane
Writer and founder of Animaline

'Cats, by their very nature, enjoy a unique relationship with humans – their independent spirits and the totally self-contained appearance they often present to the world make us feel particularly privileged when we form that very special bond with our feline friends. Small wonder then that they are such sympathetic, perceptive and treasured companions and that these qualities make them especially good subjects for healing.

'Margrit Coates, herself a great cat-lover, has a remarkable empathy both with cats and their owners. Her Soul Column in *Cat World* has generated enormous interest and positive comment from the magazine's readers as more and more people come to realise the potential benefits of healing for their pets. Margrit doesn't promise 'miracles' – although in some cases she does achieve them! Her case studies demonstrate remarkable improvements, not just to cats' physical well-being but also to disturbed behaviour patterns, in some cases releasing the animals from deep-seated fears caused by traumas which occurred many years ago. In less happy circumstances, she is able to make a much-loved pet's final day or months much more comfortable and stress-free and also help the owner come to terms with the grief of loss. Taking things one step further, the chapters on animal chakras and healing energy are inspirational, teaching us to open our minds to our pets' feelings and needs so that we in turn can attempt to work the 'magic' of healing on the companion animals who mean so much to us.'

Jo Rothery
Editor, *Cat World* magazine

'Some of the hundreds of dogs we see each year are emotionally traumatised by the life they have led, as well as suffering from physical neglect. Margrit Coates showed us how healing could help these dogs and how it can complement the care they already receive. We noticed the immediate sense of peace it brought to the dogs she treated. During the time they spent with us, their behaviour was

significantly calmer and their physical condition was seen to improve more rapidly than we would have expected. We have now started to use healing at the kennels following Margrit's initial visit.'

Sara Muncke
Chilterns Dog Rescue Society

'Margrit's incredible talent for picking up on and healing an animal's individual energy field is quiet remarkable. In this fascinating book she shows us how to connect with our pet's energy patterns. Of course, like us, animals are tuned in to specific cosmic forces. As an astrologer I am amazed at how animals faithfully express their horoscopes without words and react to vibrational forces such as the full moon. Each sun sign has a specific disposition that can easily become out of balance in an environment that lacks the vital qualities that enhance well-being.

'Here in *Hands-on Healing for Pets* Margrit explains what you can do to bring out the best in your pet's temperament and exactly how to support its individual energy and health. Astrology teaches that everything is connected. We are drawn to our pets in the same way that we are drawn to other humans. There is a mutual exchange of energy that is necessary to our understanding. Our pets have a lot to teach us. If we can receive the message of their energy field into our lives, this is an important step in our own awareness. In this sensitive and beautifully written book, Margrit shares her valuable healing expertise with us so we can learn more about how to give healing energy to our animal friends and how they are sending us theirs.'

Debbie Frank BA Hons, DF Astrol, Astrologer for *Hello*, *Instyle* and
www.femail.co.uk

'This book is highly recommended for anyone who wants to explore and consolidate the human–animal bond. Healing sessions with your animal companion will allow development of a deeper understanding of the things that make your animal unique. The closeness of the bond will enable you to detect earlier signs of disease or disharmony, often before physical signs are manifest. This book is one I would keep close at hand to be delved into at regular intervals.'

Cheryl Sears MVB, Vet MF Hom, MRCVS
Homeopathic veterinary surgeon

'A captivating and heart-warming book about the fascinating subject of healing for companion animals. Every animal lover should have this book. My own experience with healing is that it has allowed me to facilitate the course of injury recovery by releasing emotional and physical blockages which if left unheeded restrict and prevent full return to function. Physiotherapy and healing integrated together have significantly transformed the responsiveness of the tissues and allowed a deeper level to be reached.'

Amanda Sutton
Veterinary Physiotherapist
MSC Vet Phys, Cat A ACPAT,
MCSP SRP, Grad Dip Phys

'Having worked with Margrit Coates, I can vouch for her integrity and her wonderful ability. Her gift to animal healing is enormous and this book *Hands-on Healing for Pets* is yet another contribution to this important field.'

Nick Thompson BSc Hons,
BVM&S, Vet MF Hom, MRCVS
Holistic veterinary contributor for *Dogs Today* magazine
Consultant in holistic veterinary medicine

'I had the privilege of meeting Margrit Coates during her visit to the United States in the Fall of 2002. I found that experience to be extremely eye-opening. As a veterinarian neurologist and neurosurgeon, I was fascinated by her work, and her close association with veterinarians in England. She is a fascinating person whose writing and insight I find extremely intriguing. I feel that we in the healing arts professions must always be open to new ways of treating patients, be it cat, dog, horse or human. There is no doubt that by combining all our expertise our patients will be better served. Margrit's healing ability and insight certainly contribute to that effort. Her book enlightens, informs and educates people on how to better relate to animals in a supportive and healing manner. I highly recommend *Hands-on Healing for Pets*.'

Steven F. Skinner, DVM, Diplomate – American College of
Veterinary Internal Medicine (ACVIM) –Neurology, Oregon Veterinary
Referral Center, Portland, Oregon, USA

'When Margrit first told me about the brachial major chakra, or key chakra, I wondered what on earth she could mean and tried to equate it to the shoulder chakra in humans, which seemed to make sense. Imagine my surprise when I really *did* find this chakra and found the power there that was truly awesome. Like Margrit, I can find congestion and inflammation within the chakra. Since I have been working with the brachial major chakra and visualising black, I have found this chakra may be used in a similar way to how Margrit uses it – almost as a reflected chakra or as a catalyst of the others. Now I can't wait to get my hands on animals to detect even more of what I originally felt.'

John Cross Dr Ac, MCSP, SRP, MRSH
Author of *Healing with the Chakra Energy System*

The pet's healing prayer

Gently soothe me
touch me with your healing hand
fill my life with peace.
See how through these eyes
my inner light shines
to reach deep into your heart.

Listen to the energy
feel it warm you too,
for we share this earth's soul
and in healing me you heal yourself.

Margrit Coates
© 2003

Margrit Coates with Dennis, a Belgian hare

Introduction

Hands-on healing is becoming an increasingly popular treatment for animals, as more and more people realise the benefit of complementary therapies and then decide to share those benefits with their pets. Pet magazines now regularly give advice on natural remedies, and increasing numbers of veterinary practices offer a range of complementary therapies to their clients.

Using homeopathy and herbal remedies at home can be confusing (and in some cases do harm), and not many people are confident enough in their anatomical knowledge to massage their pets, whereas hands-on healing is completely safe and uncomplicated. Done with love, it can do a great deal of good. Another bonus is that it helps to strengthen the bond between human and animal. Healing energy is available anywhere, anytime, and it costs nothing. Healing can also be given by anyone, young or old, to any pet for any condition. By giving healing we are helping our pets, and this knowledge alone can be a great comfort when an animal is unwell. We can feel so helpless at such times and to know that we can actually *do* something is very encouraging.

When I became very involved in animal healing I went into a book shop to find information on the subject. The shelves in the mind/body/spirit section were piled high with books about all areas of healing, chakras, auras and meditation *for humans*. But I could not find a single book devoted solely to hands-on healing for animals, even after extensive searching on the Internet. As I was particularly involved with horses at the time, this encouraged me to write my first book, *Healing for Horses*. I have since received many hundreds of letters from people telling me how much they were inspired by the book and how using healing has dramatically improved both their own and their horses' lives.

The next step was to write this book, *Hands-on Healing for Pets*, to show every animal lover how they can not only help their pets through healing, but grow closer to them and truly communicate with them on a spiritual soul level. Healing is, I believe, the key to linking with our pets and transforming our own lives on a very deep level in the process. It opens us up to a deeper understanding of our interconnected destinies, as well as what we may learn from our pets and what help we can give them.

Best of all, giving healing to our animals really does enable us to grow closer to them. It can make dramatic improvements to their overall well being and offers them peace in times of trouble and need.

Read and enjoy as you journey along the pathway of getting to know, and understand, your pet on a deeper level.

Margrit Coates

1 My own healing journey with animals

I heard your communication,
it reached my heart
and held my healing hand.
'I am your soul,' you said
and I knew then who I truly was.

Margrit Coates

All my life, ever since my first memories of being about three years old, I have been passionate about animals and regarded them with respect for what they could teach me and what I could share with them. Over the years I have learnt from them and communicated with them and they have been instrumental in my development as a human being. I've never understood why all humans don't respect animals and why many harm them, kill them for profit or pleasure, or are cruel to them. Animals are part of our destiny and what we do to them reflects on us personally.

Even as a child I knew intuitively that humans had much to credit animals with and have a great deal to learn from them. I was somehow aware that animals play an important role in our spiritual evolution. Inside each animal, including all our pets, is a special energy being which communicates with us, but which we so often do not hear. We can, however, tap into the ability that all of us have, called the intuition or 'sixth sense' that interprets energy information and signals. Animals communicate with us all the time on this frequency and this is where communication begins and ends; we just have to listen with our hearts and our minds. Giving healing holds a very powerful 'key' to this communication with our pets – as this book explains.

The destruction of our planet and its animal life fills me with dismay for in destroying our environment the human race is destroying itself. However, there is a glimmer of hope – the return to natural therapies such as hands-on healing for animals is growing. The beauty of healing is that you don't have to worry about dosage, what to use and when, or whether or not a treatment is suitable. Hands-on healing can help any pet for any condition and is quite literally at our fingertips. Becoming aware of our

destiny through interacting with animals is a common experience for a wide range of people from all walks of life – and everyone, no matter what age or from what belief, can appreciate this by becoming an animal healer. In this way a whole new door opens for the human race as the awareness of something powerful and enchanting unfolds.

Throughout this book I try to avoid using the word 'owner' when referring to people who share their homes with pets. The word 'owner' does not reflect the huge responsibility we have to the creatures in our world in making virtually all the decisions regarding their destiny and their freedom. Where possible, I prefer to use the phrase 'animal care-giver'; other people use descriptions such as 'animal guardian', 'animal companion' or 'animal carer'.

A healing family background

My ancestors on both sides of my family had strong links with nature and with animals. On my father's side they were Celts, a people of deep spiritual connections, and on my mother's side they were farmers in East Prussia who lived according to the land and seasons. I grew up in the city of Hull but spent a lot of my childhood with my maternal grandmother, and during numerous long walks she would share her knowledge of animals, plants and herbs. She was, like my mother, an intuitive healer and so I always accepted this as normal and natural. I too developed this extra-sensory ability and I use it to communicate with animals and frequently to pinpoint their troubles.

I first became aware of this at around three years old. I can vividly remember sensing things that others couldn't, feeling heat and tingling in my hands when I touched sick animals and people, and seeing colours around them. As I grew up I usually kept all these things to myself, for I soon realised that I had unusual gifts and didn't want to be ridiculed for them. It is only in the last few years that healing has become acceptable to a wide audience. It was to be many years, however, before events in my life took me along a journey with numerous twists and turns to end up as a very busy animal healer.

My childhood pets

As a child we had a variety of dogs, and back in those carefree days in the fifties everything was more laid back than it is today and safer too.

There was less traffic, a smaller population and more space; pets led a less restricted life and our dogs played freely in the street outside our house. The dogs were very much part of the family and came on holiday with us to the seaside and helped my sister and me to dig in the sand. We dressed them in dolls' clothes, put silly hats on them and loved them to bits. No family photo was complete without the dog grinning by our side. I was ten years old when we got our last family dog. I had gone to play at a friend's house where there was a litter of puppies; one of them especially was grinning up at me. He was eight weeks old and I loved him deeply from that moment on. I called him Patch and he went home with me in my pocket – much to my mother's horror – but of course he stayed and lived to the good age of 16. For much of my childhood he was my very best friend. When I left home at 21 to work in London I cried for weeks because I missed him so much and when I saw people in the street with a dog I was inconsolable – how could anyone survive without a pet?

A rabbit's sense of humour

I've always loved rabbits ever since my sister and I were given a black and white pair. We called them Bill and Ben, and each day they were set free in a big run in the garden. However, they often escaped to eat the newly emerging plants and vegetables, as bunnies do! I remember one day looking out of the window after I'd been ill and off school for a few days and seeing a daffodil just coming into bloom. It was a ray of sunshine on a gloomy day and a promise of the summer to come. As I watched, thinking how pretty it was, Ben hopped over and with one big chomp it was gone! There are plenty of exasperating and humorous occasions like that when you have a rabbit as a companion.

A cat enters my life

I was 28 years old when I fell passionately in love with cats. It was the late seventies and, after getting divorced, I had recently moved house with my two bunnies Marmalade and Flopsy. I was at a very low ebb in my life but I soon made friends with a cat – a young grey and white half-Siamese called Casey. He was very friendly and talkative, and we would often stop and have a chat as we passed each other on the pavement. I also began to notice that the house the cat came from was in darkness for days at a time. Obviously the family were away a lot and, as he was

losing weight, I started to feed him. One snowy evening I came home late to find Casey huddled by my front door looking ill. I confronted the couple where he lived and was told that the woman was pregnant and that they were moving house shortly. Casey was unwanted, so I gathered him into my arms and took him in to give him the first of many healing treatments. He lived with me for the next 15 years until he died of cancer. Luckily Casey had been raised with rabbits and immediately became friends with mine, having a lot of fun together. Casey became a very close friend and, being a typical Pisces, was very much in tune with all my moods. He was a great lap cat, especially when I was troubled. That little cat brought love and companionship into my life, which stopped me from feeling lonely. Casey had tremendous healing powers and his strength was very beneficial to me. He began to teach me what being with an animal soul mate really means. Little did I realise that I would become hooked on cats and spend the rest of my life a cat slave!

A borrowed dog

Sometimes we get very close to an animal for which we are not directly responsible. At the time that Casey was converting me to being a cat person, I got very friendly with a neighbour who had a dog called Sam. Sam was a large German Shepherd cross, and at first glance he looked very fierce. He had come from a rescue centre as a puppy and was much loved by his family. He was very protective towards them, and the first time I knocked he barked and growled, throwing himself against the door to let me know he was in there.

Over a period of time I started to offer to take Sam for walks in my spare time, and I began to learn from him about a grown-up relationship with dogs as opposed to a childhood one. As children we tend to regard dogs as playmates and, when needed, also a listening ear. When we get older the playmate element takes a secondary role to enjoying exercise with them, but the listening ear is just as important, and during difficult times we can make a conscious decision to absorb their strength and empathy towards our needs. At these times a dog can become our focus as they ask for nothing in return for our love – only love. They are easy friends to be with when we are surrounded by humans making complex demands. To say that Sam became my healer is an understatement. He knew everything I was thinking to the extent that if I had the thought, sitting in my house, that I would go over to his home to take him for a walk he would get up and wait for me. His 'mum' Anita would often

phone me to ask if I was coming over because Sam was sitting by the front door – unfailingly I always was getting ready to do just that! During our walks I would tell Sam all my news, both good and bad, and discussed all my dreams with him too. This was very healing for me and in his presence I felt so much better. Of course, healing is never a one-way journey and I regularly gave my own healing treatments to Sam for various ailments. These were incredibly moving times because we were so very close to each other.

When I moved away after nine years, he was an old dog and our walks had become very short due to his arthritis. I missed his company very much when I left the area and sadly he died not long afterwards. I often think of those special walks and private talks and I feel Sam's powerful presence with me to this day. I know he often draws close to offer his wisdom when I am giving healing to a dog. He always was – and is – such a happy person. Some people may find it strange that I use the word 'person' about animals, but inside each body is an individual personality, no matter what the species. Each life is unique and valuable for its distinctive essence. I believe we should never look at animals as a collective group, any more than we should humans, because then we are in danger of missing what animals have to teach us.

Time to explore my healing

A couple of months after I had got to know Sam, and Casey had come into my life, as part of turning over a new leaf (and perhaps because cat ownership made me even more sensitive than I already was), I decided to develop my spiritual side. I had been aware of a strong healing sense for years and I felt I now had to explore what it was all about. I also strengthened my intuitive abilities, but I knew that I wanted to use these skills for healing and not for some frivolous purpose. It was this gift that I would put to good use as an animal communicator, but on a healing level. For example, I don't think it's relevant to my work to pick up communication about what colour a food bowl is, but I can receive information on how the pet feels and where the energy is out of balance.

After I finished training as a healer, I did voluntary healing work at weekends and in the evening, but I felt as though I was marking time. However, those years were invaluable as in order to be able to work well, a healer needs to have lots of practice to build up a sufficiently strong personal energy, and also the stamina to work deeply in the energy field of both humans and animals.

Time to return to my healing roots

It was a very long time before things changed and I was able to devote myself to healing full-time. When I left college I had started a successful career in advertising and PR, but as the years went by I frequently felt niggling pangs of discontent. I always felt that one day I would return to my healing roots, but didn't know when or in what way. Then the company I worked for suddenly made me redundant and I celebrated my liberation – although it was scary at the time too. I retrained in complementary therapies and opened a clinic, but after a while I became inundated with requests to give healing to animals, so I decided to specialise in that field.

Around that time I got together with veterinary physiotherapist Amanda Sutton and homeopathic vet Cheryl Sears and we started Holistic Pets – a clinic offering natural therapies for animals. Over the years I've given healing to a wide range of animals, including cats, dogs, horses, ducks, chickens, rabbits, cavies, parrots, sheep, cows, goats, wild animals, alpacas and even a camel! I've travelled far and wide with my

AN UNUSUAL HEALING REQUEST

The most unusual request I've had for animal healing came when I was at an RSPCA fund-raising event. It was a very hot summer day and two girls aged about seven or eight years old came up to the display stand that I was sharing with my colleagues from Holistic Pets. 'We've come for the healer,' said one of the girls and I noticed that she was carrying a small basket, although I couldn't see anything in it. Stepping forward, I asked how I could help. The girls put their basket down on the table and pointed in to it. They told me that Hoppy had hurt his leg and was not moving. I then noticed a small green grasshopper with a missing leg sitting on a face cloth. The girls had found him near their picnic table and having heard their parents talk about my work had decided to bring him over to me. I explained to them that healing would not make the grasshopper's leg grow again, but that it could help him to feel better. The two girls watched intently and solemnly as I held my hands over the grasshopper. After a couple of minutes Hoppy started to move around and crawl over the cloth. The two girls beamed at me with big smiles and I was very touched when one of them whispered, 'Thank you.' I told them to take the grasshopper somewhere shady and cool and let him go back to his family. The girls then trotted off happily together, holding the basket between them, over to the long grass to set him free.

animal healing work and have had some wonderful experiences. I remember once sitting in the kitchen of a country house belonging to a famous pop star after I had given healing to his dog and eating chocolate cake that had been sent to him by an equally famous Italian opera singer as a Christmas present! I am now doing something that I find incredibly rewarding and satisfying and it really is good to spend so much time with these different animals in such a wide variety of places.

We are all animals

The first animal that I came into contact with many years ago as a child helped me begin on my healing journey, and all the creatures who have crossed my path since have given me knowledge and understanding. They have all been my teachers of healing. Animals are not just physical beings, but emotional entities too; we need to remember that we are all animals – albeit in different shapes.

I believe that more people today are realising this, and desire to return to a better understanding of the universe and nature, and to redress some of the balance that mankind has upset and which affects all life on all levels. Hands-on healing works at the very core of the energy of this life.

‘Healing is a journey of spiritual communication between you and your pet’

2 What is hands-on healing for animals?

> You are led through your lifetime by the inner learning creature, the playful spiritual being that is your real self. Don't turn away from possible futures before you are certain you don't have anything to learn from them.
>
> Richard Bach, from *Jonathan Livingston Seagull*

The title of this chapter should really be 'What is hands-on healing for animals, birds, fish, insects, in fact, for all forms of life?' – but that would have been far too long! Usually the first question I am asked by someone wanting to know more about healing is 'What is it?' Healing works for all forms of life, even plants and trees, because everything living consists of measurable energy. Our pets' bodies, like our own, have the ability to self-repair but often this process doesn't work very well. It is becoming increasingly recognised by vets that the pet's emotional aspect plays a key role in this. The aim of hands-on healing is to kick-start the body into regulating itself and to smooth out all physical, mental, emotional and of course spiritual disturbances. The words 'energy' and 'energy medicine' have become buzzwords of the new millennium, but there is really nothing new here. Healing works by connecting with energy fields.

Hands-on healing is the oldest form of natural therapy, dating back to the dawn of history. Historical documents from numerous cultures contain references to healing. Two-thousand-year-old Vedic texts describe universal energy and how this can be channelled deep into the body's cells through energy centres called chakras. In Egyptian temples the priests are known to have used the laying on of hands to give healing to the sick. The Ebers papyrus, dating from 1550 BCE, mentions healing by the laying on of hands for pain relief, something that is still frequently practised today. The Ancient Greeks also practised healing to treat medical conditions. Pythagoras, the Greek philosopher who lived in the sixth century BCE, coined the term *pneuma* for the energy associated with healing. His followers believed that energy was composed of opposites, negative and positive. This is similar to the traditional Chinese

medicine philosophy of *yin* and *yang*, the dual energy states that need to be in balance for mind, body and soul harmony. Disruption of their balance is said to adversely affect health and feeling of well-being. This balance is also vital for the health and well-being of our pets, and indeed all animals. The Greek philosopher Hippocrates noticed that healers produced sensations of tingling and heat, which was accompanied by the relief of their patients' symptoms. He concluded that healing energy is the vital force of life, something that today's scientists continue to research. Later on throughout Europe, kings practised healing and throughout many cultures the touch of the hand to comfort the sick has continued.

Neither is the understanding of life force energy new – many long established medical philosophies share this concept for healing. Eastern medicine refers to this life force as *ki* or *chi*. Western medicine has over the years neglected the life force and failed to acknowledge its existence. An animal, just like a human, needs to be helped on all levels for general health to be truly improved or restored. Exploring healing takes us on a rich and wide learning journey. Once we start, we never stop learning about both our own and our pets' energy fields.

Hands-on spiritual healing is not veterinary medicine or a substitute for veterinary medicine; it is a natural therapy that anyone can give if they so wish – as natural as a mother holding the hand of a sick child or kissing it better. For many people, their pets *are* family members and close friends, and the emotion invested in them is enormous. Healing is another way of being close to them and getting the best out of our relationship together.

'Every living thing is made of energy. Everyone has the potential to influence another being's energy system. With intention, the healer influences energy systems, aiming for even flow'

Hands-on healing – a straightforward approach

I am a down-to-earth person and like to keep everything straightforward and easy for all to understand. It is my opinion that over the years the concept of hands-on healing has often become over-complicated, thus all too often making healing exclusive and inaccessible to most people. One of the many typical letters I have received was from a man who read my book *Healing for Horses*. He said, 'Until I read your book I never thought that I would live long enough to understand what healing was all about or that I could be a healer.' My aim in this book about healing for pets is to explain the subject in a way that enables people to realise that healing is for all of us. It is often called spiritual healing because it works with the life force of the individual body, whatever the species.

I see so many new courses and therapies advertised that appear to be just re-inventions of straightforward hands-on healing. Many therapies rely on subtle energy connections within the body to create beneficial changes, but surely when this happens it is simply healing in its purest form. Healing doesn't need to have a new set of rules, an attention-grabbing title or complicated ceremonies. With true healing there are no rituals, symbols or dogma to come between you, the healer, and your pet, the receiver. Healing is there for everyone to access and no one can lay claim to having invented it or discovered it. Healing energy has been part of our world since the beginning of time and belongs to each one of us who chooses to be a healing rather than a hurting person. There is no hierarchy to follow with healing; the relationship is a personal one between you and the source of the healing energy. I believe that the more complicated it is made, the less effective it can become. Healing is done on a one-to-one basis – involving an exchange of energy between the healer (yourself), the one receiving it (your pet) and the creator (the spiritual source). It is a safe, gentle and non-invasive therapy.

It's quite astounding what knowledge and skills our ancestors had, which we seem to have lost along the way. They knew that energy exists in and around humans and animals, and indeed in all life forms. Over the years more than 150 studies have looked at healing and the changes and benefits that can be produced. Healers visit hospitals, hospices, clinics, veterinary practices and animal charities around the world and many healthcare professionals practise healing as well. Because hands-on healing is so simple to give, and anyone with the right attitude can do it, it is often overlooked or not considered as an option. Surely it can't be that easy? Yes it is – and when you start to do some healing with your pets, you will realise just how easy and very effective it can be.

The healing touch

Using the hands for healing is normal and natural. Animals use their paws, bodies, noses, and even their presence to comfort each other. Apes and monkeys have always touched each other, reaching out in a healing way with their fingers to relatives and friends when they are troubled. The desire to touch a person or animal that is unwell is a natural instinct, but there is more to healing than just touching. When we touch with the actual intent of giving healing, as opposed to an absent-minded stroke or pat, we make a powerful energy connection and communication. During

> ### Defining spiritual healing
>
> The word 'spirit' refers to the life force or vital essence of a living being, so to describe our life as spiritual means tuning in to our non-physical part. This is a personal process and religious beliefs are not necessary. Animals, because they are so sympathetically adjusted to nature, tune in to non-physical aspects all the time. Spiritual healing therefore means healing the vital essence of a person or animal. This life force is the soul energy.
>
> The healer is the channel for the spiritual source of universal healing energy. This source provides what is needed to match what is missing or out of balance in the pet. The energy is directed through the life force or vital essence of the animal by the good intent of the healer. Healing can work physically, mentally or emotionally. The pet takes what it needs at that time and the healer has no control over this, but through love offers general healing help.

healing, our hands are used to facilitate beneficial energy changes in the life force or spirit of a human or animal.

Giving healing is something very special and very powerful that we can all do to help our pets. We don't even have to know that there is anything wrong to be able to benefit a pet with healing, as we often don't realise that they have a problem. This is because they can't actually *talk* to us about how they think and feel. When an animal begins to show signs of illness, it may in fact have been feeling unwell for some while. In my experience, when offered healing animals are generally very willing to let go and to move on if possible.

The link

Everything on earth is connected and every life is part of a greater whole. We all share a common energy, although within that we have our own individual energy signature, as do our pets. Nothing is without significance and what affects one life, no matter how small or how far away, will reverberate through the universe and affect us all. This is another reason to choose to become a healing rather than a hurting person. Of course, we might not take part in hurting directly, but we can do so indirectly by buying products or foods that have involved animal abuse and exploitation in their production. Therefore it's part of following a healing pathway to avoid such things. Our own energy will be much healthier, stronger and brighter for it too.

A mysterious force

Healing aims to rebalance the complex energies within cells, which interact to work together for the benefit of the pet as a whole. The healer uses his or her own electromagnetic field to channel the healing energy. However, healing is a good deal more than an adjustment of energy. It is a link to something extra that actually creates the changes – a powerful, potent and mysterious force which is greater than mankind. What is this force? I don't believe that anyone has a real understanding as to what it is or where it actually comes from. Because animals are highly attuned to nature and are very sensitive, I believe that they probably understand this force much better than humans do. I often look deep into the eyes of animals and see an awareness that evades humans. I think how wonderful it must be to have their connection with the universe and nature in general, to understand the energy of the moon, the tides, the wind and weather, to respond to an inner homing instinct and to feel the magnetic field of the earth. Even the smallest insects have so much more knowledge about these things than humans have and this knowledge is vitally important for our future. How much distress the human race causes these beings by interfering with their world – and ultimately everyone's world.

Is faith necessary for healing to work?

Faith in terms of religious belief is not necessary for a person to be a healer as it is a non-denominational therapy. I really hate the term 'faith healer'. The personal faith that I have as a healer is that the animal will know I wish to help it on whatever level is possible. However, I personally do believe in a power that I call God as the source of the healing in its widest sense, but I do not follow a particular religion. I mix with people from a wide range of beliefs, cultures and nationalities and find that I have something to learn from all of them in my fascinating journey to understand the origin of healing energy. Many organisations and individuals over the years have either repackaged healing as something new or surrounded it in mystique so that it seems inaccessible. Religions also have often tried to keep healing as some sort of secret system, attempting to guard the use of invisible healing energies so that they are available only to a chosen few. Although healing energy is a mysterious power, the use of it is not a mystery – it is available to all of us.

Animals have absolutely no concept of human faiths and belief systems and understand only the forces of nature and its relationship to the universe as a whole. They are naturally in tune with the healing power and that is enough for us as healers to link with them. Research has shown that when healing is given it can be effective, no matter what background or belief either the healer or the receiver has. Where the source of the healing lies no one really knows. From the beginning of time people have pondered on this question and looked for an answer. It really doesn't matter where you think the healing comes from, the source is the same. Whether you think it comes from angels or the stars, for example, it is the desire to help (healing intent) and the loving thoughts (healing focus) that matter. So whatever our background or our beliefs, the healing energy is there for us all to quite literally get in touch with.

'All healing takes place at soul level'

Scientific evidence for healing success

When you browsed through the book, this chapter may have been the section you looked at first to see exactly what healing is all about. Many people contact me to say that they are sceptical but desperate so are willing to try healing, hoping for the miracle that will help their pet. Healing is not a miracle cure – all physical life ages and degenerates and we must look at healing in the context of that fact. However, healing is a very powerful therapy and there are many documented cases of the dramatic and sudden benefits that it can produce, both for humans and animals.

Until fairly recently scientists were fairly sceptical about the claims made for hands-on healing. However, over the years a great deal of research has been done with healers. This has produced proof that healing works and that it uses energies. We now know that the energy field coming from the fingertips of healers scans and swings backwards and forwards in a similar way to the medical pulsed electrotherapy machines used to treat bone, muscle, tendon and ligament injuries. When giving healing, our own energy field is constantly transmitting all of the frequencies needed by the patient, whether human or animal, but – unlike using a machine – these will constantly vary both the level and intensity of their vibrations to match the body's needs. Healing goes one step further though, because healing energy also helps to activate the release of deep memory and emotional blockage in the tissues. Many times I have given healing to animals who have not been responding very

well to other forms of treatment because they needed deep emotional help too.

Remember, the actual healing energy does not come from us but from another source somewhere in the universe. Tuning in to the pet's energy field successfully is something that some people find easier than others. Because I do it all the time, for me it is very easy; within seconds of touching an animal, I'm working with subtle movements, vibrations and sensations. It's a bit like the violin player who can pick up an instrument and play a fine tune without thinking about it or reading any music. I cannot play a violin but I can detect energy fields and fine-tune them. Until you try healing you don't know how much of a maestro you will be; people frequently tell me they are pleasantly surprised once they do have a go. Your pet will certainly benefit from it.

Some healing research

Studies into healing confirm the existence of an energy exchange between the healer and the receiver. Elmer Green, a well known American researcher with the Menninger Foundation in Topeka, Kansas, enclosed healers in electrically isolated rooms whose walls were made of pure copper so that all electricity from other sources would be blocked out. He demonstrated that during healing sessions surges of up to 100 volts registered from electrometers placed on the healers' bodies – an increase of over one thousand times the norm. Video footage taken during the experiments confirmed that these voltage surges had nothing to do with any physical movements made by the healers. Green published a paper about these experiments in 1991 and this famous piece of research has become known as the 'copper wall experiment'.

Numerous laboratory studies have been carried out with both animals and plants to study the effects of healing. In a classic experiment in the 1960s, Canadian Bernard Grad demonstrated that seeds watered with a solution treated by healers grew much more vigorously and had more chlorophyll than seeds given 'unhealed' water. Other experiments showed that rye seeds grown with water held by healers had a four-fold increase in the number of new shoots. Parapsychologist Dr Serena Roney-Dougal has carried out lengthy trials at an organic farm near Glastonbury in the UK, which confirm that healing energy has the ability to enhance and protect. In her trials, published in 2002, lettuce seeds treated by a healer consistently resulted in a ten per cent increase in yield and were more healthy than seeds which weren't exposed to healing

The healing touch is a powerful energy connection. During healing, surges of up to 100 volts are emitted from the healer's body. Healing energy transmitted through the hands scans and pulses in waves as it reaches through the body of the pet on whatever level is possible.

energy. It appears that people who love nature can make a healing connection which they transmit from their hands every time they touch something. When people see my garden they often ask me what I feed my plants to make them grow so abundantly – 'Healing,' I answer!

Following a series of lengthy and complicated experiments involving healers and enzymes in California in the early 1970s, Dr Justa Smith concluded that the energy fields of healers produced a variety of changes in different types of enzymes, which encouraged improved health of cells, and that healing could even repair damaged enzymes. Enzymes are proteins that act as biochemical catalysts and play an important role in the body. Speeding up enzyme reactions helps the body to repair itself. This experiment alone therefore demonstrates the influence that healers have on cellular function, which in turn affects the whole body. This applies equally to our pets and shows us how beneficial healing can be for them for a wide variety of conditions.

Scientists have also proved that healing energy has a tendency to increase haemoglobin levels in the blood, which in turn strengthens the

immune system. Haemoglobin carries oxygen to the body's cells from the lungs and carbon dioxide away from the cells to the lungs. We can see by this that improved haemoglobin function through healing plays a vital role in improving health. In scientific studies undertaken with animals and healers, hands-on healing was shown to increase the rate at which wounds repaired and became healthy tissue again and healing given before surgery stimulated faster recovery from operations. Other studies with animals demonstrated that healers can slow down the growth of cancerous tumours. I have myself been able to help pets with this condition many times. These examples are just a sample of the great number of studies conducted into hands-on healing.

The placebo effect

When I was specialising with healing for human cancer patients, sceptics would argue that there was a placebo effect whereby very sick and frightened people so desperately wanted to feel better that they imagined that they were better. I accept that there may on occasions be an element of this placebo effect with humans, but this argument doesn't hold up at all with animals. Quite simply there is no placebo effect with animals.

CHEWY

Chewy would easily pass for a lion if you saw him. In fact, if you saw him loping through the meadows with his two companions, you would be forgiven for thinking that you were in Africa. Chewy is a Leonberger dog, so named because his ancestors came from the French town of Leon. He was just ten months old when a vet recommended that I see him for healing treatments. Even at that young age Chewy was bigger than most adult dogs, but was also incredibly gentle and from those eyes shone a good and kind soul. Chewy had just come back from a veterinary hospital where he had undergone major surgery to repair a torn cruciate ligament to his right knee. Six weeks complete rest had been ordered, which was very difficult for such a young dog. His time was spent in a cage in the kitchen, let out a couple of times a day for short periods of exercise. For several months he was only allowed to walk and not play, run or jump. To make matters worse, the prognosis was not good for the other leg either – the vets said that there was a 95 per cent chance that it would need surgery too. And to cap it all, hip dysplasia had shown up on the X-rays. The reason for the healing was two-fold – to help speed up the repair of the

damaged tissue and to help the dog emotionally and mentally because of the enforced restriction.

When I saw Chewy the first time he was a sorry sight. He was in some pain despite the strong painkillers, and he looked depressed as well, not surprisingly. He was panting, although the room was cool (a sign of pain), and his eyes were dull. Over the months I was to see those eyes brighten and shine with happiness. Chewy was already lying on his side and as soon as I put my hands on him he seemed to know why I was there. With a big sigh, the dog lay his head down on the pillow I had brought with me to kneel on. I didn't have the heart to move him so he stayed on the pillow and I knelt on the hard floor. Chewy very quickly responded to the flow of healing energy – he became motionless and his eyes stared ahead with a soft expression and then he drifted into a deep state of relaxation. After a while there were several twitches in his muscles as pent-up energy was released. Then his care-giver Pam noticed that several parts of Chewy's body were becoming hot. In my experience these 'hot spots' occur where there has been infection or inflammation in the body and where the healing energy is clearing the blockage away. At the end of the treatment Chewy was asleep and did not move, even when I left the room.

Chewy was so unwell that I saw him weekly for a month, then reduced the treatments to fortnightly. He was a text book case to treat and absolutely loved his healing. When I arrived he would greet me with a big fuss, then go straight to the place where I gave him healing and lie down waiting for me. Over several months Chewy continued to improve and got stronger, but we were concerned that the other leg would give way and have to be operated on. However, it didn't, and Chewy got well enough to go for long walks and to play with the other dogs.

After a year Pam took him back to the veterinary hospital to be X-rayed again. A few days later the results came back – not only was the left leg not in any danger of giving way and requiring surgery but no sign of hip abnormality was noted. In fact Chewy was given the unbelievable hip score of 2/2, excellent in such a big dog. (A hip score is a measurement of hip abnormal development and the nearer to nought the better. Some breeds are prone to hip problems, which can lead to lameness. Dogs with a score of above 6 should not be bred from as problems can be passed to the puppies.) The next day Chewy was let off the lead to run around the woods as much as he wanted to, and since that day he has proved just how strong his limbs are. He has jumped in rivers, climbed mountains, swum in the sea, and chased his doggy friends over the meadows, leaping and twisting in all directions, and bounding along full of energy and life. Pam tells me she puts the dog's amazing recovery and improvements down to the regular healing that he had.

Animals naturally understand and respond to healing for what it is and what it does for them, not because they anticipate any benefits or because they feel reassured by the therapist. Healing is a great leveller and the response from animals the proof – if indeed any more were needed – that healing works.

The four brain wave states

Through our healing thoughts we activate the healing mind – this is our innate intelligence. Our thoughts create energy states and changes within the brain, which scientists can measure. The mind, however, cannot be measured; no one actually knows where it lies but within it lie all our thoughts, each with an individual energy pattern. Mind energies exist outside the physical body and when we concentrate to give healing we make a mind-to-mind energy connection with our pet that influences the brain.

The brain produces four frequency ranges – alpha, beta, delta and theta. Usually people don't have all four wave states operating at once, but it has been shown that healers do because of the deep meditative concentration and relaxation that they achieve when giving healing. This is known as the 'awakened mind', and the more that people practise healing, the easier they find it to reach this state. Interestingly, during a healing session the alpha brain wave patterns of both the healer and the receiver synchronise. These synchronised brain wave patterns then further pulse in unison with the earth's magnetic field – called the Schumann resonance after the scientist who discovered it. I find that many animals 'plug in' to the healing and reach the alpha state very quickly, obviously enjoying the energy sensations within their bodies and minds. A cat's purring has been found to be on the same energy frequency as the alpha wavelength. Animals, as well as humans, vibrate at an energy rate and emit brain wave patterns. Animals are affected and influenced by the energy resonance that is caused by our state of mind and attitude. This is why strong healing comes from a calm, dedicated and selfless approach.

Healing hands and energy fields

Scientists know that changes can be detected from the hands during healing treatments. Pulsing magnetic fields, for example, are sent out from the hands and these scan through the animal to help on whatever level needs it. Often when I have my hands on a pet, their care-giver will tell me that as they touch or hold it they feel a sensation 'like a pulse' in their own hand. I reply to them that is exactly what it is! The healing energy pulses as it responds to the body's needs, and as people pick it up they will feel this come and go, growing weaker or stronger, and then they may not be able to detect it at all as cells balance.

Another very interesting fact about healing is that during a treatment the biomagnetic or energy field coming from the healer's hands increases by at least 1,000 times greater than normal. It is possible to measure our own biomagnetic field from our hands. This aura of energy from the hands can be photographed in a process called Kirlian photography (after the Russian scientist who invented it). Through noting disturbances in the energy readings corresponding to areas of the body, Kirlian photography can also show where there will be problems in the *future* before any symptoms start to appear. When a problem appears it is often a while after the energy field has become out of balance and so healing given regularly can help the body to correct itself rather than produce a disease or illness state. Healing works by rebalancing the complex pattern of energies, which is why it is good to give it as a preventative measure to our pets rather than just waiting for a problem to appear.

Just like our own, our pet's energy field consists of a very complicated network and all the components are constantly responding to and influencing each other. The body's energy is a combination of

Healing energy fields

Energy fields surround all living beings, including our pets. These fields change and adapt constantly, depending on what is happening either physically, mentally or emotionally. They give us a picture of what is happening within the pet. When we give healing we release blockages within the energy field, aiming to achieve a more even flow where everything works in harmony.

Energy can be many things and it can be a combination of things all happening at once. It can be volatile or calm, move with either a positive or negative polarity, and be constructive or destructive. When energy is destructive or negative it becomes volatile and changes body tissue for the worse; when it is constructive or positive it has a calming power and can influence body tissue for the better. Within body tissue flows the subtle mental and emotional energies – and of course the energies of the soul.

pulsing fields and the main components are electrical, magnetic, gravity, thermal, light, kinetic and sound. During healing we deal with all of these wavelengths and get results according to which level is responding, as well as the pet's particular problems. All the body's energy fields are scientifically measurable, as are the energy states within individual organs and cells.

Healing the whole body

Healers usually treat on a general level because the symptom or trouble spot may not be the source of the problem. Treating holistically allows the body to take the healing energy wherever it is needed. The actual source of the problem may lie deep within the animal and could have been triggered off by an event a long time ago – even many years before the current condition appeared.

🐾 Healing aims to strengthen a pet's inner resources and achieve a complete balance, called homeostasis. The idea is that the body will be stimulated to repair or stabilise from within, both physically and emotionally. All illness and disorder will have involvement with an emotional level in some way.

🐾 During a treatment energy is transferred via the healer to the animal and travels down lines of energy in its body. These lines of energy may correspond to chakras and meridians or they may not. You can actually place your hand anywhere on an animal and make a healing connection, but there are some areas where the connection can be

Chakras

Chakras are energy centres found in various parts of the body. They relate to physical, emotional and mental health. Chakras act like gateways through which energy enters and leaves the body. Each chakra has its own colour component and the major ones together make up the colours of the rainbow. Chakras are linked to each other and have a negative and positive polarity – a balance between each one is vital for good health. Our hands can feel the flow of energy from the chakras and sensitive individuals can also see the colours emitted from them. Animals have bigger, brighter chakras in relation to their body size than humans do. Chakras and their benefits are described more fully in Chapter 6.

Meridians

Meridians were named by the Chinese and are energy highways or pathways along which the vital energy force, a specialised nutritive flow to the organs of the body, flows. They are also low-resistance pathways for the flow of electricity. Meridian channels extend right through to the heart of each cell in the body. The layout of the meridians forms the basis of treatments such as acupuncture in eastern medicine. Scientific research into acupuncture reported in the *Journal of Chinese Medicine* has shown that meridians emit light energy which can be seen using infra-red photography. Hands-on healing can be given along the meridian channels as well as through the chakras.

---

stronger, such as the chakras (see Chapter 6). I often target specific areas for healing, based on my experience and the pet's condition or where I can see that the aura is blocked. The aura is the area of energy around a body and this energy vibrates at different speeds. The wonderful thing about healing is that when we give it to our pets we are creators of beneficial and positive energy. The pet is helped to release destructive and negative energy into the universe for it to deal with.

Detecting animal auras

Around every living creature exists an aura – an electromagnetic field containing all the information about that being. It is this information around a body that we sense when we say that someone gives us good or bad vibes. Our own energy field is either disturbed by their energy or feels in harmony with it. It is the same with the aura given out by animals. Clients often comment about the occasion when they chose their pets that as soon as they walked into the room a particular animal attracted them, even if it was not what they had been looking for. Something about the animal triggered off inner feelings of compatibility, which made them want to take the animal home. Animals are also very sensitive to each other's auras and this is something that we need to appreciate and make allowances for. Just as we don't click with every human we meet, it is the same for other creatures if they find an aura disturbing in some way or another. When we are faced with this situation, healing can be used to help the auras of all concerned become more harmonious.

The aura

The aura comes from within the body and records what is happening to a person or animal at any given moment. The word aura comes from the Greek word *avra*, meaning breeze, because it can be felt but not normally seen around a body. Like chakra energy, the aura is composed of physical, mental, emotional and spiritual levels of being. The aura is made up of a number of layers and can extend some way out from the body. As we become more sensitive to the energetic levels of a body, we can detect the aura quite easily, either seeing the colours it produces or sensing the patterns with our minds. The energy level of each chakra is represented in the aura. The state of health can be analysed by the purity of the aura colours – vibrant colours are a sign of good health, while muddy and dull colours are a sign of poor health. The colours of the aura change constantly, depending on the emotions being expressed at the time.

The etheric body

The etheric body connects the vibrations of the spirit, mind and soul energies with the physical body, rather like a bridge. 'Etheric' comes from a Greek word which means above the clouds, because at death the etheric body may be seen to rise out of the physical body by sensitive individuals. The etheric body appears to mirror the shape of the physical body as it contains the blueprint of the physical energies, both from past experiences and current conditions. The chakras connect the etheric body with the physical body.

Electromagnetic fields

An electromagnetic field surrounds and penetrates the physical body in all living creatures, influencing what happens on the physical level. This field of energy seems to have polarised qualities, such as positive / negative and north / south. The electromagnetic field can be filmed and photographed. Studies of electromagnetic qualities have shown that they are associated with channels and energy points throughout the body.

Similarly there is also an energy field radiating outwards from the earth, which is called the geomagnetic field. With both humans and pets, it is important to exist in harmony with the earth's natural electromagnetic field for optimum health. The more we are in tune with nature, the more we harmonise with the universal energies of which we are part. When we interfere with the natural lifestyle of a species we interfere also with their harmony with nature. Hands-on healing helps us to get in touch with the resonance of the earth and to become one with the universe and all the life it contains.

The aura radiates colours. I frequently see this field as a dense band of yellow light when I am giving healing to animals. If there are dark places I know that is where there are problems. It is possible to see colours or patterns in the aura as well, and these will change as the healing progresses. Some individuals find it easier to see human auras and others animal auras; I fall into the latter category.

A gift for everyone

Healing can be used anywhere and for any condition. It can be used to treat on a general level or to target specific things such as an injury. Everyone is different, with their own strengths and weaknesses, and some people will be able to develop greater healing sensitivity than others. The sensations can be very subtle and some people will be able to feel, sense or even see them more than others. Sometimes we may be more 'in tune' with one animal or species than another as our individual personalities play a role. However, even if the giver is unable to 'feel' anything, the healing will still be effective on some level. The act of giving healing is the most important thing. Healing is a gift offered to everyone but some people will have a natural flair and aptitude for it. Practice and training will produce confidence, develop skills, and broaden understanding and knowledge of the process of healing.

Healing attunement

I believe that when we are born to this earth we arrive with the permission to heal, and that we are already attuned to the healing source. Attunement is the linking, or resonating, with the energy of the person or animal we are giving healing to. All we need to do is make the connection from within ourselves to our pet. Each person can give healing if they really want to by tuning in to their higher self.

Focus and intent

There are two vitally important things we have to do if we want our healing to connect and be effective. We have to really *want* to make a difference and we have to *link our thoughts* with the animal. This is called our healing focus (thoughts of help) and healing intent (wanting to help).

The brain is responsible for all the body's functions, but it is in the mind that our thoughts originate and exist, and each thought has its own energy signature. The energy of the mind exists separately from the physical body. When we focus our thoughts to give healing, we actually connect with the thoughts of our pet – its mind – and it connects with ours. This connection lets the animal know that we wish to help and so it is comforted by this intent of ours.

Important elements for healing: unconditional love, positive thoughts, empathy, engaging in soul energy

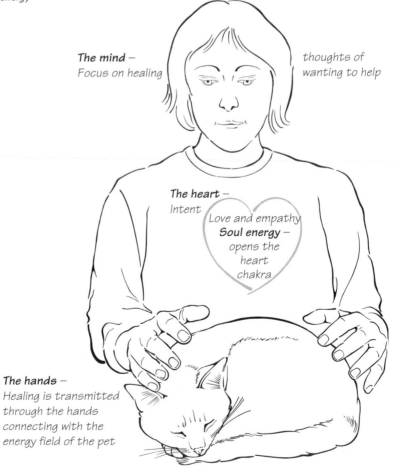

The mind –
Focus on healing

*thoughts of
wanting to help*

The heart –
Intent

Love and empathy
Soul energy –
*opens the
heart
chakra*

The hands –
*Healing is transmitted
through the hands
connecting with the
energy field of the pet*

Our healing intentions are not just trivial words or thoughts – science has demonstrated that they produce certain patterns of electrical and magnetic activity in the nervous system. These patterns of energy spread from the healer into the body of the person or animal being given the healing. Intention to help and thoughts of love will have a positive and beneficial influence; uncaring, selfish thoughts will have a negative and detrimental influence.

'Thinking healing' creates a powerful means of attaching our electromagnetic field to that of our pets, so that the healing that is needed is channelled through our hands and the communication of what they need begins to be heard. Giving healing is a living prayer and it raises the energy of all creatures, not just the one we are working with, and the world in general. The healer benefits by being enriched through the unselfishness of healing, by the love it generates and by the good it does. We start to listen with our inner being, our true natural self, and rediscover the skills that the human race has neglected and ignored.

Mind energies in all living beings exist for eternity and when the body dies they live on. Unlike the physical body, the energy body cannot be destroyed, only converted from one form to another. The thoughts of animals who have suffered and lived in distress and in terrible conditions create a darkness in the world. Animals who have known love and have been cherished send beams of light to guide us. The mind connections that we make when the pet is with us remain attached forever as streams of positive energy and universal light. These streams of light also travel to help other animals in need. Giving frequent healing to something we love and cherish helps the energy of this world generally and the healing is also beamed to every cry for help. There are millions of cries for help every second, so isn't this the very least that we can do for all those creatures so reliant on the human race who have no freedom to live as nature intended them to?

'Energy follows the direction of thought'

Healing is a great leveller. Animals judge us not for our clothes, what car we drive, how expensive our house is, or what we look like. Material wealth often causes people to feel either superior or inferior in comparison to others. The currency of healing is unconditional love and that is priceless. Animals see our aura and look into our soul; they sense whether we are spiritually rich or poor.

39

BOOTSIE'S MIRACLE

I first got chatting to Michael about cats and healing when he was up a tree. My cats watched him from a bedroom window, mesmerised that he had gone so high up into the branches. The tree was a huge willow and Michael was a tree surgeon who had come to prune it before it took over the garden. We talked about a mutual love of all animals, my healing work and about our cats. Michael and his wife Molly lived a couple of miles from me so I said, 'If ever one of your cats is in trouble, call me and I'll do all I can to help with some healing.' 'Touch wood,' Michael replied. 'They're all fine at the moment, but I'll bear it in mind.'

Eighteen months later the phone call came. 'We've just got back from the vets with Bootsie. She's very ill and they wanted to put her to sleep, but we just couldn't bear it. We've brought her home.' Five minutes later I was at their house. Bootsie is a chunky black cat, and was then nine years old. She lay on the back of the sofa and was obviously very poorly. Her eyes were filled with blood and she looked uncomfortable and hunched up as cats do when they are ill. The vet had diagnosed acute kidney failure from blood tests taken earlier that day and when they advised euthanasia Molly and Michael went into shock. Just two weeks earlier, Marmalade, their beloved two-year-old cat, had been put to sleep for the same reason. They felt pressurised and didn't give permission this time so hastily – they wanted to bring Bootsie home to say goodbye and to cope with the shock. The vet told them that there was nothing more that they could do and if the cat lasted the night to bring her back in the morning for euthanasia. They agreed to the cat having healing.

I explained to Molly and Michael that healing was not a magic cure-all, and no promises were made about the outcome. I was aiming to give Bootsie peace with the healing. They understood. 'That's all we want for her – but I can't help wishing for a miracle,' said Michael as he stroked the little cat. Carefully I placed my fingertips over Bootsie and began to give her healing. Very quickly she started to respond, flexing her paws and stretching them out to acknowledge that she was feeling something – that she was feeling the healing energy. Michael and Molly stood by Bootsie with their eyes closed, obviously sending out their own healing thoughts. Bootsie started to arch her back into my hand and then I could hear a soft purr. It was a sure sign to me that she knew that I was helping her with the healing and that she wanted as much as she could get. Suddenly she rolled onto her side and stretched herself out, looking comfortable and at peace. 'Look at that,' said Michael. 'She really looks happy now.' When I left she was sleeping and did indeed look very happy.

The next day I went back to be told that Bootsie had got up in the morning and asked for some breakfast and, although very weak, was definitely

brighter. She lay on the back of the sofa and again, as I gave her healing, she pushed her body into my hands. Her purring was louder and at the end of the healing session she stretched out long and relaxed like a cat should be. Two days later Bootsie was eating well and walking around, and the bleeding in her eyes had stopped. Every few days over the next two weeks I called in to give healing to Bootsie and she continued to improve. I explained that as well as offering pain relief and helping tissue repair, healing could also have a detoxifying effect and that is what must have happened in Bootsie's case. The day that I dropped by and the little black cat wandered off as I sat down next to her, I knew she didn't need me any more. It was her way of saying, 'Thanks but I'm OK now. Go and give your healing to a cat that needs it more than me!'

By this time Bootsie was going outside again. Molly and Michael delighted in telling me at great length what she was up to .She had been running along the shed roof, eyeing up the mice in the stables and climbing the apple tree. Molly and Michael had registered with a new vet who looked at the blood test results from the previous practice, confirming that Bootsie had been very ill – in fact, the tests showed that her kidneys were failing and she should not really have survived that night. 'She's a miracle,' the vet said. Bootsie was prescribed some long-term medication to help prevent further problems and to assist the kidney function.

That terrible time was over two years ago and Bootsie is still very well. Whenever I see Michael and Molly they point at Bootsie playing in their garden and say, 'She's our little miracle.'

Convincing the sceptics

I am used to people who are very sceptical about healing watching me work, but rarely do they remain unconvinced about it afterwards. A few such cases spring to mind. More and more vets are training in complementary medicine, both to fulfil client demand and to satisfy their own desire to do the very best they can holistically. Like doctors, many vets are suspicious of the benefits of healing, but there are now vets training as spiritual healers. In fact, some have attended my own courses.

I received a phone call from a young vet called Jane who had been qualified for about 18 months and who told me she wanted some inspiration to move forward in her veterinary career. She described herself as a very sceptical vet but open to new ideas. Although Jane was

'Everyone has the free will to either heal or hurt – it is as simple as that'

a companion animal vet, I took her to a horse yard, as the visual results of healing with horses can be very dramatic for onlookers. To her amazement Jane spent the morning discovering her own hands-on healing abilities and helped treat one particularly depressed mare. As we drove home she was full of questions for me and said that she had indeed found the inspiration that she was looking for. There *was* some great force of energy out there in the universe, she said – she had witnessed it and experienced it that morning.

'The energy doesn't come from you,' Jane said.

'No, I know,' I answered. 'It comes from a higher level of consciousness, some divine source in the universe. But how do you know that?' I asked her.

Jane replied, 'I could feel it in great waves and it was like a buzzing pressure in the air. When you put your hands on the horses it started and when you took them off it stopped.'

It was her professional opinion that healing created, or stimulated, a synergy within the whole body. It is always good to get people to describe their experiences and it is confirmation for me as to how healing works.

Jim came to me at the Holistic Pets clinic on referral from a vet with his German shepherd dog Flyn who was epileptic. He sat down and stated that he had come because the vet had suggested that it was a good idea but he was very sceptical. His wife 'believed in such things', but Jim went on to explain that he was a person who could only deal in facts and things he felt for himself. You can't put healing in a bottle or a pill, so Jim had difficulty in understanding it. As I lay my hand on the dog's back to begin the healing, I caught the look of sheer scepticism on Jim's face – it said, 'Well, I'll do anything to help my dog, but really I think I'm wasting my time.' After a few minutes I could feel a flow of healing energy through my hands. Flyn was showing a typical response. He looked sleepy and sighed a couple of times, laying his head on his paws. I looked up and Jim was watching me with the same look of doubt on his face because to him it looked as though I wasn't doing anything at all, other than just sitting there resting my hands on his dog! 'Put your hands gently here on Flyn,' I said, 'and hopefully you will feel something.'

A couple of minutes later Jim started to flex his fingers. 'I think it's my imagination but my fingers are starting to tingle.'

I told Jim to put his hand back on to the dog and when I had completed the rebalancing so that everything was working in synergy he would feel his hand pushed away from the body. Gently he laid his large

strong hand on the dog. Time went by and I lost myself in the peace of the healing and then I felt everything change – homeostatis or balance had been completed. I looked up to see Jim's face had gone red and his hand was shaking. It was about two inches from the dog's back, whereas a few minutes before it had actually been resting on his back.

'You can't keep your hand down, can you?' I asked.

'No, I can't,' he said. 'It's being pushed away from Flyn's back.'

He went even redder and gasped as he tried to keep his hand down. Suddenly he pulled his hand away. 'How did you do that?' he demanded. Jim had experienced the healing energy and its power. His scepticism had not blocked the experience. Jim was a man with no faith whatsoever, but he left that day with plenty to think about. Jim hadn't seen the healing in a bottle, but he *had* felt it and it had been *more* powerful than his physical strength.

Some people I come across, however, tell me that they don't believe in healing because they tried it once and it didn't work. Often people have unrealistic expectations from healing. One lady I spoke to told me that she was a sceptic – she *knew* that healing didn't work because of her own experience. She'd had a rabbit with myxomatosis and called a healer in, but the bunny still died. This terrible disease is a killer and healing is not magic, neither can it reverse traumatic tissue damage. It amused me that this lady was still prepared to consult her vet for her pet's problems, even though he had not been able to cure the bunny, but not a healer ever again. Perhaps she misunderstood what healing was about. One thing I do know – the bunny would have received the benefit of tremendous peace from the healing.

Healing benefits for pets

Healing:
- is safe to use for any condition and has no harmful side-effects
- is a natural therapy reaching not only the physical body, but also the mental and emotional levels
- works with the pet's own inner resources aiming to achieve balance
- stimulates cellular and tissue repair where possible
- helps with pain relief
- can be both calming and stimulating
- can produce an improved sense of well-being and a feeling of inner peace
- helps other therapies to work more deeply.

3 Why pets need healing

All beings are spirit – energy patterns that emanate from the Source/Oneness. Just like ourselves they exist as soul. . . . There is no animal therefore, however small, that is not open to and does not respond to healing. The whole area of spiritual healing with all types of animals – not just pets, horses and other domesticated animals – is waiting to be explored.

Jack Angelo, from *Spiritual Healing*

Animals are intelligent beings and are naturally very capable of learning due to their own natural devices. They are capable too of intelligent thought, and have an emotional state, as research is now proving. Above all, they have individual characters. Our pets are really wild animals at heart, and have evolved to become domesticated (over many thousands of years in the case of cats and dogs, for example) and be taken into our homes. Throughout our lives we are subjected to a range of factors – both good and bad – that influence us, such as upbringing, education, diet, hereditary factors, climate and weather. Pets are affected by a range of things too, but if something does not suit them they cannot usually make lifestyle changes. We make the decisions about their lifestyle and take away their freedom to make choices and be totally themselves. That's when things can go wrong, however well-meaning we are. We've all made mistakes in our lives, myself included, but we did the best we could at the time, based on the knowledge we had. When we know a better way, we need to act on that knowledge.

Each species is different in its needs, character and behaviour, all of which have been influenced by millions of years of evolution. What seems reasonable, even instinctive, behaviour to an animal can appear unreasonable to us humans, and is the cause of much misunderstanding. There are fundamental differences between animals and humans, and many problems occur because these are not taken into account. Pets suffer from physical problems just like we do, and living a human-created lifestyle can trigger many conditions, including emotional problems. Animals are very sensitive to human moods and

to atmospheres in the home environment. This complex soup of energies can be very unsettling for them and will affect their own emotional and mental state. Nancy and her dog are typical examples of this, referred to me for healing because of skin problems. Tests had found nothing conclusive and the vet thought that, as the care-giver had some family problems, this might be affecting her dog. Nancy told me that she had suffered a recent bereavement, and also that her teenage son was jealous of the attention she gave to the dog, which

Electromagnetic fields radiate out from every living being, overlapping and blending with each other. Through these energy states flows body/mind/soul information and gives us a readout of positive or negative vibes about other people and animals. Hands-on healing aims to calm the shared energy field of both human and pet. Via our energy fields we can magnify and reflect our problems onto our pets and vice versa. Reflecting our problems or moods onto a pet can affect its well-being.

stressed her. I could sense during the healing that the dog was worried about the care-giver, and she in turn was worried about him. The two of them were reflecting emotionally disturbed energy backwards and forwards between them, which intensified it. I joined them both in the healing to clear their shared energy field and the result was a calmer human and consequently a healthier dog.

Healing reaches all the complex areas and the aim is that it will help you and your pet to understand each other better as your energies blend and you communicate on a much deeper level. In this chapter I explain some of the areas that can influence pet health and behaviour and hopefully give an insight into changes that may be needed. I also explain why pets need healing and how it affects our relationship with them too.

Healing is suitable for any animal and for any condition. Thankfully it is being increasingly acknowledged as having a vital role to play in a wide spectrum of animal health and welfare issues. Whenever I read in the newspapers about an animal that I feel would benefit from healing, I write to explain how healing could help. Often I do not get a reply as the recipient probably thinks that the suggestion is far-fetched.

I saw a story about a baby hippopotamus at Dublin Zoo who was grieving dreadfully because his mother had suddenly died and as a consequence he was spending a lot of time under water – he was quite literally trying to drown his sorrows. I immediately wrote to the zoo director and was delighted to get a letter by return telling me that since the story appeared in the press the hippo baby had begun to recover due to lots of extra attention from the zoo handlers. I was further very heartened to read in the letter that they believed in the benefits of healing. They had recently moved an adult male orang-utan to Rhenen Zoo in the Netherlands on a breeding loan. The recipient zoo was very concerned as he had become severely depressed and despite loving care from the staff was not responding. To their credit, they consulted an animal healer to treat him. Within a week the orang-utan was his normal self again and as a result of the dramatic change the story was widely reported by the Dutch media. This demonstrates the power of healing to reach deep emotional levels in animals to help them feel more at peace.

Animals can suffer from stress just as much as humans do. In the wild some stress is necessary to enable the animal to learn how to survive, defend itself, find a mate or seek food. With captive or domesticated animals, stress due to a restricted or unnatural lifestyle, boredom, overcrowding, lack of exercise and stimulation, incorrect diet, over-breeding, grief, fear of humans or abuse leads to a very unhealthy

> ‘ Negative thoughts create chaotic and unbalanced energy and will result in a poor healing connection ’

and unhappy animal. Your pet may have suffered from some of these conditions before you got it, so it is good to give healing to help it let go of all the negative memories and to strengthen the immune system.

The emotional pet

There are many things that as an animal healer I've taken for granted over the years, not least that I thought that everyone recognised that all animals communicated emotions, thoughts and feelings which are just as valid as ours. People have said to me, 'But they are just animals and you are humanising them. They can't be described in the same way.' I ask them why they believe that pain, fear, anger, grief, envy, loneliness, boredom, compassion and love can only be experienced by humans. I have looked into the eyes of too many animals during healing sessions to know that these are not exclusively human feelings.

For years scientists have put pets into categories and types, ignoring the real issues concerning animals because the complex emotional state wasn't recognised or considered. Things are now changing thankfully as behaviourists are identifying animal emotions as playing a fundamental role. The same applies with animals as with humans, in that their problems will have an emotional link even if it is only in part. Animals are quite up-front about showing their feelings too – interpreting them correctly and making the right changes is often the difficult bit for us humans.

Scientists have been able to demonstrate the effects of emotional stress in animals. In one particularly unpleasant experiment mice were exposed to two different types of stress. One of the groups was given electric shocks to the feet; the other group was forced to watch a mouse being given a shock to the feet. Both groups had free access to morphine, which is both mind- and pain-numbing, but only the mice who witnessed the torture of their friends, i.e. were subjected to severe emotional distress, self-administered the morphine. This shows that the emotional stress rather than the physical stress made the mice more receptive to the benefits of the morphine. It appears that animals can cope better therefore with physical stress rather than emotional stress. If creatures as small as mice can show such emotion, then this suggests the depth of feeling that bigger animals, including horses, dogs and cats, will have.

Dogs can also become emotionally stressed because they are left on their own by their care-givers. Zoologist Dr John Bradshaw, director of

> ❛Positive thoughts create harmonious energies and are used to make a positive healing connection❜

47

the Anthropology Institute at the University of Bristol UK, has stated that for some dogs the care-giver departing from home can break their hearts. Pedigree dogs are known to suffer the most, especially Labradors and retrievers. With these stressed animals, Dr Bradshaw advocates seeking advice from a qualified animal behaviour therapist via a vet. 'Owners need to realise just how crucial is their role in creating animals that are emotionally robust and that can cope with modern life,' he says. Interestingly, Dr Bradshaw found that cats are less dependent than dogs on their care-givers, but that they suffer from emotional anxiety in other areas of home disruption such as when the layouts of rooms and furniture are changed.

Time and again I am asked to give healing to animals whose coping mechanism has failed because they have become emotionally blocked. I can only imagine what it feels like to be an animal, unable to speak and communicate their turmoil and distress to humans, and too often being punished for communicating their frustrations in their own way.

Animals' minds

All animals have mind energies and mental states that can be healthy or unhealthy. These are not conditions exclusive to humans. Like humans, they have a psychological aspect too and can suffer from mental illness and exhibit disturbed behaviour for similar reasons, including over-crowding, lack of stimulation, boredom, insufficient exercise and too small a territory. Caged birds pluck out their feathers in distress; overstocked fish become upset and sick, swimming frantically around; bored cats and dogs can be destructive or toilet inappropriately in the home; and rabbits kept in hutches for most or all of the time are in a prison. Rabbits are among the most neglected pets in terms of adequate freedom and, unlike most cats and dogs, are silent when distressed. No rabbit will be happy if it is kept in a hutch all day – they need access to a large run or even to the house (watch the electric cables and phone wires, though!), as they can be litter-trained. Animals definitely have minds and the more socially developed ones such as cats and dogs have quite complex thoughts and emotions too.

When a pet is affected by something, either emotionally or mentally, it may get blamed for bad behaviour or it can suffer from ill-health. What it is doing, however, is communicating that something is wrong. The animal can then become exhausted and depressed, with a depleted immune system leading to health problems as its energy field spins out of

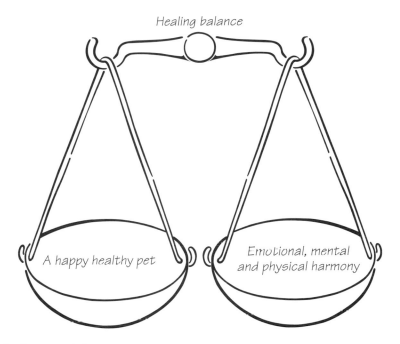

Healing balance

A happy healthy pet

Emotional, mental
and physical harmony

The healing energy balance

balance. The problems may be long-term (chronic) or short-term (acute), but all will affect the energy field and have a knock-on effect over a period of time. Future events will be influenced by the disturbances, depending on the individual pet's ability to cope with things. These are all reasons why pets need healing. I hope that by now you are beginning to understand how everything is related and how complex animals are – just like us. After any kind of stress, problem or upheaval in a pet's life, giving healing is always a good idea. First, however, we need to see if there are changes we can make to resolve the problems the pet is communicating to us.

To be truly healthy, a pet needs to be physically, mentally and emotionally balanced. Healing plays a major role in this respect as it reaches all of these levels at the same time.

The senses

Animals' senses of smell, hearing, taste and direction are far more sensitive and acute than those of humans. Imagine the frustration and anguish it causes them not to be able to function fully as nature intended. Animals are very sensitive to touch as well, and can feel even the tiniest

insect crawl over their bodies. Providing stimulation and as natural a lifestyle as possible for pets is vital to their overall well-being, and a pet kept in an unsuitable environment will be very miserable. An animal's sense of sight affects how it relates to the outside world too – birds, for example, are stimulated by bright colours.

Animals' acute sense of hearing can cause them distress in noisy places. Sound in its negative form can cause imbalance in the body. Disturbing sounds include hard rock and rap music, heavy traffic and repetitive noise, such as machinery or engines, etc. Birds who live near motorways, for example, lose the sweetness of their song and also find it more difficult to attract a mate. Fish and sea mammals are being increasingly traumatised by noise pollution from ships and water sports – and whales are known to be losing their sense of direction.

Research has shown that increased stress in an animal can be caused by exposure to loud noise including pop and rock music. Queens University in Belfast undertook a study on behalf of the National Canine Defence League and found that whilst classical music helped to reduce stress in dogs, heavy metal and grunge music resulted in more aggression, depression and fatigue. Animals can also suffer from headaches caused by tension just like we can. Clinical researchers have studied how such noise can unbalance basic organ function, leading to a weakened immune system which in turn can lead to illness and disease.

Sound in its positive form helps reduce blood pressure and includes classical music and, of course, the sounds of nature, such as bird song, stream water and gentle breezes. Animals also respond to music therapy and some veterinarians play calming music in their clinics for this reason.

The root of the problem

When I give lectures or demonstrations I ask people to tell me what the animal standing in front of them is and what they see. They look puzzled, wondering what I mean. I can almost hear them thinking, 'It's a dog, a cat, a horse. . .' or whatever it is I'm working with. Then I tell them, 'This is a person that looks like a dog, a cat, a horse. . . .' Animals are blood, flesh, bone and nerve endings, just like we are – what we feel, animals can feel too. However, animals don't use words to communicate their problems and have no freedom to change their circumstances, and this is often where the problems start. Many of the problems from which pets suffer are related somewhere along the line to human intervention,

mismanagement or lack of understanding. That isn't to say that a current care-giver is necessarily doing something wrong – the root of the problem may have happened before the pet was acquired.

Healing helps us to get to know our pets on a deeper level because by becoming healers we aim to develop a sensitivity to energy

Wherever I go, cats and dogs are drawn to the healing and will appear to bathe themselves in the radiated energy. They often settle down close by to take what they need as I work with another creature. Life-force energy radiates out from all living creatures and there is no point at which it stops, although it gets weaker the further away from the body it gets. Healing energy can be sent an unlimited distance to help any animal in need.

51

communication and our intuition or 'sixth sense'. The healing touch then allows us to receive feedback from our pets, and this can work so deeply that it subtly enhances the relationship from both pet and human viewpoint for the better. I have found that the more healing we do, the more we can tune into these subtle earth energies and so can make lifestyle adjustments to help not just our pets but ourselves too.

The environment and geopathic stress

If the pet's environment is creating havoc, then healing will not be as effective as it can be. We need to be aware of the whole picture to see if there are any possible changes that we can make. Building materials in our homes and electrical appliances can have a disturbing influence on pets. The World Health Organisation, for example, recognises sick building syndrome as a cause of health problems.

Environmental factors may be damaging the delicate balance of our own energy field too. There are two types of harmful radiation, that which occurs naturally in our planet and that which is created by mankind. These are called geopathic stress and have been found to be a common factor in many serious and long-term illnesses and psychological conditions. We know that all life is affected by positive and negative ions in the atmosphere, just as we know that cosmic forces change the speed of many of the biochemical processes in not just our own but our pets' bodies.

An important influence is the Earth's natural radiation field, which is both good and bad in places. There are also electromagnetic wave changes caused by underground streams, rivers, springs, mineral deposits and ley lines. Every living organism reacts to these in one way or another. However, the responses vary – plants and animals can be divided into two groups depending on how they react. There are those that thrive in areas of geopathic stress above subterranean watercourses and those that, like human beings, find such areas intolerable and instinctively avoid them. If that is not possible they can become ill. Cats, bees and medicinal herbs thrive in areas where the earth's energy activity is high over underground water sources. Bees are even known to produce more honey above underground streams. However, dogs, horses, rabbits, rodents, reptiles, birds, cattle, chickens, pigs and most other domesticated animals will naturally avoid these areas of disrupted energy.

- Cats are attracted to areas where the Earth's energy activity is high. They absorb negative energy and want to relax people. That's why they are drawn to people who dislike them – they want to soothe. Energies blend and interact with each other, and some animals – like some people – have energy fields that respond in certain ways to Earth energies in order to create a more balanced energy environment in that particular area. Bees and termites are also drawn to these areas of negative energy, which makes them more active and productive.

- Dogs, horses, rabbits and rodents, reptiles, birds, cattle, chickens and pigs will naturally avoid areas of disrupted energy. They are drawn to areas where energy is in harmony and operates smoothly with an even flow. No one knows why certain animals avoid areas of disrupted energy and others are drawn to them.

- Fish are very sensitive creatures and disturbance in energy is transmitted through water and can cause them to suffer. They do not have mechanisms to deal with these disturbances.

Electricity pylons, telephone masts and other such structures emit low-frequency radiation, which has been linked to health problems. It's not advisable to take dogs walking near sources of radiation, such as electricity stations, pylons or nuclear power stations.

EARTH STRESS STORY

I visited a couple who have a variety of animals. I was told the horses didn't like their summer paddock and stood at the gate all day. They wouldn't drink from the trough, but would rush in at night to drink in their stables. I learned that the dogs would only run round one edge of the field and the chickens rarely went in it when they were free to roam. The big clue came when I looked over the gate and saw a large tabby cat sunbathing in the corner under a hedge. I asked if anyone knew of underground water in the field. The reply confirmed my suspicions – there was a filled-in well in the corner where the cat was, and the horses' drinking trough was on top of it! Everything then made perfect sense. The animals were all acting according to their natural instincts and following what was right for their needs – something we all too often misunderstand. The owner moved the water trough, sectioned off the field and planted fruit trees in the corner where the underground well was. The animals were much happier. Using their new knowledge of earth energy, the owners also put some beehives over the well and now have lots of organic honey.

With caged pets or fish suffering from health problems, try moving them to different places to see if that helps. They may just be in an area of earth energy disturbance. Cages, pens or fish tanks shouldn't be placed near electrical appliances, fuse boxes, generators, televisions or computers, as these all create electromagnetic radiation.

It is important, therefore, that pets should have a choice of places to rest and sleep so that they can link with nature as it suits them best. It's better for pets if they can have free choice to avoid rooms they do not wish to spend time in.

Weather and the seasons

The earth has elemental energies relating to the seasons and the weather, and they are measurable in water, air, fire and the ether (the aura of energies from all living things, which contains the blue print of life). Scientists can detect and quantify the components of these energy areas and the continuing changes that take place, depending on the circumstances. For example, the balance of negative and positive ions in the atmosphere changes according to the weather. Weather-sensitive people can suffer from health problems just before changes in the weather, such as headaches, limb pain, sleep disturbance, fatigue, confusion and indigestion. It is known that animals' electrical fields alter in advance of weather changes, which demonstrates how natural forces affect them – yet how little attention we pay to it all. Recently I noticed that my two young cats were madly hyperactive throughout the whole of one night – it was a full moon and in the morning there was a thunderstorm.

In my experience certain types of weather or different seasons also affect energy connection when giving healing. Sometimes if there is an electrical storm brewing, I may choose to keep the healing session short, especially if giving healing to animals kept outside. Sensitivity to energy changes is part of the complicated soup of disturbance that healers can pick up on when treating animals.

Chemicals in the home and garden

In today's world we are bombarded with products which fill our homes and gardens with hundreds of toxic chemicals and pollutants. These products include furnishings and floor coverings, cleaners, air fresheners, disinfectants and detergents, insecticides and herbicides. As well as being potentially damaging for human health, these chemicals are equally unhealthy for pets. Pesticides have even been linked to Parkinson's disease in humans and have produced similar symptoms in animals. As the effect of chemicals in pesticides breaks down the immune system, this contributes to the overall ill-health of the animal, including being a contributory factor in epilepsy.

Animals are much closer to the ground than we are and so can inhale more fumes from cleaners and sprays in the home, and toxic substances on the ground in the garden. Pets can suffer from skin irritations as well as breathing problems due to chemical reactions. Dry air in over-heated, poorly ventilated houses (double glazing can be a culprit here) can also cause ill-health. Birds can easily be poisoned by the fumes from cookware and fish can be poisoned by sprays used in the house that settle on their water. Pets kept in homes where people smoke inhale the fumes and in effect become passive smokers, so plenty of fresh air and ventilation is essential for them.

Diet

Often a pet's health and behavioural problems are linked to their diet. Pets may be allergic to the unnatural additives, preservatives and colourings that many foods contain. These allergies can cause behavioural problems, such as aggression and hyperactivity, as well as physical health problems. A growing band of holistic vets are recognising this and advising that a natural diet is the best, including raw foods for cats and dogs. Dental problems and obesity are on the increase and are frequently diet-related. It is a good idea to consult a vet to advise on the best diet for your pet. If what is being offered does not fulfil all the needs for that particular type or species, then the whole balance of the body will be affected and the healing you give will not be as effective as it might otherwise be.

Light

All life is attuned to the daily cycle and rhythms of sunlight and the seasons. Daylight is a vital force and it's recognised that for optimum health we need a balance of the seven spectrum colours which daylight

contains. Light is one of the wavelengths in a body's energy field and our healing will connect more quickly if that wavelength is not depleted. Pets can suffer from lack of daylight in the same way as humans can, becoming depressed, lethargic and even physically ill as a result. Going outside for even just an hour a day improves overall well-being. Full spectrum light can dramatically improve animal health too when they are ill. In a recent study the life span of hamsters with heart disease was enormously increased when they were exposed to full spectrum light for 24 hours per day. This shows how other sick pets too can benefit from good natural light.

Natural daylight is at least five times brighter than standard artificial lighting and we can make changes in the home to benefit both our own and our pet's health. Fluorescent or strip lights send out pulsing vibrations, which set up a resonance within the body and can cause restlessness and irritability. However, there are special lamps available which produce light that closely resembles the balance of natural light and the quality of daylight. It's a good idea to ensure that pets have access to bright areas of the house or are allowed outdoors as appropriate. Cages, hutches and pens should not be constantly left in gloomy places. Exceptions are those pets whose natural requirements include dark or semi-dark environments. Dogs usually go outside to walk and play every day, but sufficient natural light for indoor cats can be a problem – even more of a reason to provide them with a secure outdoor area in which to exercise. Weather permitting, birds will enjoy access to outdoor aviaries, rather than being just confined indoors in cages. Rabbits, of course, naturally live outside and those kept as house bunnies do need fresh air too.

Whatever the animal, always make sure that they have access to cool and shady areas away from the sun or weather when they go outside. With the more unusual pets, it's essential to take expert advice about whether they can, or should, spend some time in outdoor areas to benefit from natural light.

> The healing connection follows the love in our hearts

Water

Water is as important for the health of our pets as it is for us and is nature's most essential medicine. Water isn't just to quench thirst; it lubricates all the cells and tissues, regulates body temperature, is vital for proper digestion, and removes toxins and bacteria from the body. Water also transports nutrients and oxygen around the body. If the body

contains good levels of water, then healing benefits can be more intense as water has been proven to transport energy.

If your pet is not drinking enough, it will affect not only its health but also its energy field. If you think that your pet is not drinking enough (or starts drinking more than normal), contact your vet for advice. We can't recommend to our pets that they drink more, but we can make water more appealing to them. Many pets dislike the taste and smell of the chemicals in tap water, so filtered or still mineral water may be more acceptable. I find that offering the cooled water from a boiled piece of meat to dogs and cats encourages drinking as it makes it more tasty. The type of drinking bowl can be relevant. Plastic gives off fumes and can be scraped by pet's teeth – stainless steel and heavy ceramic dishes are better. With drinking bottles for use in cages it is vitally important that they are kept scrupulously clean.

Company

For many of the species we keep as pets, company is vital as in their natural state they would live in groups. For dogs and cats, adequate human company can keep them happy. Often keeping two cats or dogs together is a good idea though, or may be important in some cases. Animals can get as lonely as we do and behavioural or physical health problems can manifest themselves as a result. Bored dogs and cats create activity to bring relief from the boredom. This excitement floods the system with addictive chemicals so they keep repeating the behaviour. The answer is not to punish but to understand them better and relieve the boredom. Other pets including rabbits, guinea pigs, rats, mice, gerbils, birds, and fish need to be kept at least in pairs (same sex) to keep them emotionally stable. Your veterinarian can advise on any neutering necessary. On the other hand, there are certain animals, including hamsters, who do not normally tolerate being in company. Advice should always be taken from a specialist about the best lifestyle for any pet.

Socialisation and weaning

The early days of a pet's life, notably for cats and dogs, are vitally important in terms of how their personality will develop and how they will interact with humans. Rabbits do not need to be handled

SNOWY

Snowy, a large white bunny, was found abandoned and shivering in a cardboard box by a rubbish tip. It was just chance that someone unloading their car looked in the box. She was very thin and the vet said that she was lucky to be alive, and for a while it was touch and go as she was treated in the local animal hospital. I gave Snowy healing several times over a couple of weeks to help her, and each time she would become very still as my hands gently touched her. After a couple of visits she got to know me and would climb onto my lap and go to sleep, then suddenly wake up and furiously twitch her nose.

With the help of the healing and the peace that it offered her, Snowy started to trust humans again, becoming a real favourite, and after a short while she was found a new home. Although during the healing I had picked up images of a small dark house with lots of cats, the rescue centre didn't want to try her with them as she had been through such a lot of stress already. Snowy went to a quiet bunny home in the country where she was to have a huge outdoor area and access to the house.

Not long after she arrived a neighbour's large ginger cat, Pickles, was seen entering the house through a window. Snowy was inside taking her afternoon nap and there was panic as the family ran in wondering what they would find. The cat was sitting in the middle of the room and Snowy was sniffing his nose, then she casually lay down on her side by the cat as if she had known him all her life. Snowy was obviously a cat person! Pickles was a very laid back chap and he started to wash his paws in a most unconcerned way. After that day Snowy and Pickles spent many afternoons together in perfect harmony, both enjoying the companionship.

particularly from a young age and with love and patience can make good pets when acquired as adults. It's a vastly different story with cats and dogs, however, and many problems that care-givers are faced with stem from inadequate socialisation by the person who bred them. Being brought up by a breeder in a cage or pen, either indoors or outside, is not acceptable for kittens and puppies as they are missing out on their essential socialisation needs. Many pets I give healing to for emotional dysfunction have not had the correct start in life. Without a doubt the best home to get puppies and kittens from is one where they have been raised in a family environment with plenty of human contact, freedom to play and explore, and introduction to all the normal household noises.

Puppies and kittens need to be handled and petted every day by a variety of people. Scientists know that there are crucial times when kitten and puppy socialisation should take place. For puppies this period is between two and 16 weeks and for kittens between two and seven weeks. During this time, being stimulated (experiencing different humans and animals, hearing a variety of noises, being taught how to cope with frustration, exploring new areas, smells and textures, etc) consolidates connections in their brain cells, the majority of which can only be made during this period. If they miss out and are not stimulated enough they will be less able to cope in later life. There is a huge variation in responses between different species and different breeds within those species. The correct start in life means that the pet can learn to identify with its feelings and therefore respond better to us when it is an adult.

Unless advised by a vet, pets must not be weaned (leave the mother) too early – kittens and puppies learn important socialisation lessons from their mother and their littermates and early weaning can cause emotional and behavioural problems in adult life. Ideally puppies, kittens and baby rabbits should not be taken away from the mother before eight weeks of age.

Pedigree problems

Many of the pets referred to me for healing for serious health complaints are pedigree breeds, and it's a well-known fact that certain breeds of cats and dogs are prone to particular problems. These not only cause distress to the animal, but also to their caring human partners. I am horrified by what some breeders around the world are doing to distort the bodies of cats and dogs in the pursuit of prizes and accolades *for themselves* – you only have to look in a specialist pet magazine to see what I mean. Good breeders are interested in producing animals who are healthy and not misshapen. Time and again I see stressed people with pets suffering a lifetime of problems owing to defects. Many of these animals need veterinary treatment and hands-on healing throughout their lives.

Your vet can advise you on what problems are now inherent in which breeds and what to look for as a sign of good health or as an indicator of potential problems. For example, too narrow or too flat a head/face affects the teeth, breathing, eyes and sinus; too narrow hips can affect the bladder and digestion; long bodies and short legs affect the

joints and spine – the list is endless. Fancy titles and famous names are not the primary thing to look out for when buying a pet – an honest love and empathy for the animal's long-term needs is the number one priority in choosing a breeder.

Space

All pets need stimulation and plenty of room to move around. Lots of pet problems stem from lifestyle difficulties and unless these areas are addressed the benefits of healing will not last for more than a day or two. In some cases, the healing may not even be accepted by the pet at all. The world is fast becoming an increasingly dangerous place to live for both people and animals. In many areas it is not safe to let cats roam, and in some places it may not even be allowed. However, it is an imprisonment to a pet if a run, cage or pen is too small to move or fly around properly, and there is no variety in life. Sometimes the pet's distress is obvious when it becomes destructive to its environment or even attacks its own body. At other times a pet may become severely depressed; it may just appear 'quiet', but is suffering just as much emotionally and mentally.

A while back I went to visit an acquaintance. The first thing that she said to me was, 'Isn't it a beautiful day? Let's sit in the garden.' She never let her cats out and I felt uncomfortable sitting in the sunshine while they watched from the window. One of them had been rescued and was used to going outside previously and it communicated to me its deep sadness and frustration. Fortunately soon afterwards the garden was specially fenced so that the cats could go outside but were safe as they couldn't leave it. The joy that they now express at the variety of life around them, and their freedom in being able to sniff the flowers, hide in the bushes and lie in the sunshine, is indescribable. Another client had a dog that cried all night as soon as she put it in a pen at bedtime. When she stopped doing this, the dog chose a place where it was happy to sleep and didn't cry any more – understandably it had hated being locked in a cage.

However, cage and crate training under the supervision of a pet behaviourist can have many benefits for insecure and phobic dogs who need a 'den' to feel safe in. Many dogs who have been crate-trained depend on them and a lot of dogs will choose an enclosed area as a den to sleep in. Pets appreciate a choice of safe and familiar areas to rest in as they know best what their needs are.

Specific conditions that healing can be used for

Because it works holistically, healing can help with any condition, reaching the mental, emotional and physical levels within the body. Healing is the basis of balance or even flow of universal energy within the body and can be used alongside all medications and therapies.

Because healing creates such a sense of peace it is good to offer it regularly, even to pets without any health problems, just because it creates such a pleasant feeling of well-being. Remember, hands-on healing can be used preventatively to help keep everything running as smoothly as possible. However, be sure to ask your vet for advice about anything that concerns you before giving your pet healing.

> **Important!**
> Hands-on healing should never be used as a substitute for veterinary care and advice. Always consult a vet for any concerns regarding a pet's health or wellbeing. Changes in behaviour can be a result of pain, illness, disease or depression.
>
> Healing cannot reverse severe organ or tissue damage or degeneration – there is a time span for the physical life to end for all things.

These are some of the ways and conditions with which healing can help.

- The pain relief benefits of hands-on healing have been well documented. Healing releases endorphins in the body, which are nature's own painkillers.

- Healing offers natural pain relief for arthritis and joint problems.

- Healing can do no harm to a pregnant animal and is soothing for the mother.

- With problem births, healing can be used both for the new-born and mother.

- Changes of ownership or home circumstances can cause stress or depression. Healing has the potential to calm in these cases.

- Healing has been known to lift the spirits of depressed pets and improve their general well-being.

- Healing offers inner peace for emotional disturbances.

- Pets can be hyperactive before and after epileptic fits and seizures. Healing aims to calm the animal and help its body recover and cope with the cause better. Epilepsy can be volatile but because healing is safe and offered through our love it will not aggravate it.

- Animals can become very sad and depressed if a human or animal friend is no longer with them. They can be affected by grief for a long time. Healing offers comfort and balance to grieving animals and helps natural remedies to work more deeply.

- Pets get headaches just like we do for a variety of reasons, including neck and back problems, fevers, injuries, poisoning, allergies and liver or kidney disease. Healing can help by offering a better balance of energy to allow other treatments to function more fully (see Chapter 12).

- Healing, by rebalancing energies, can have a detoxifying effect to help with liver and kidney problems. This may be quite marked on occasions with the releases of toxins from the body. Pets can become much brighter as the organs are stimulated.

- Pets often become unsettled, worried, jealous or even angry at new arrivals in the home, whether people, babies or animals, and abnormal behaviour may result. Healing aims to help a pet to feel more confident and relaxed.

- Healing is therapeutic for elderly pets.

- Healing has been shown to help boost the immune system.

- Healing helps an animal deal with previous ill-treatment, no matter how long ago this was. We can talk about our problems or cry, but our pets cannot. Healing helps release negative energy from the past, offering a feeling of inner peace.

DODGER'S HEART PROBLEMS

Dodger is a handsome collie dog of the old fashioned English type rarely seen these days, with a large well-proportioned head and a strong body. Dawn has ten collies, including Dodger, as she breeds and shows them. The dog had been born with collapsed heart valves, first detected when he was five months old and at nine months old he had a cancerous tumour removed. Dodger

hadn't been expected to live very long, but here he was eleven years later with his only other problem being bad arthritis.

Five days before I was called to see him, Dodger had had a heart attack in the garden. He had suddenly looked unwell, then collapsed, and was rushed to the vet for treatment. After all these years of Dodger living with such a serious heart problem, Dawn feared that the dog was due to die at any moment. She thought that healing could help Dodger with his problem, but I explained that I couldn't make any promises about a physical recovery. I explained, however, that healing also works emotionally and that he would be comforted by it. Certainly Dodger did not look at all well, his eyes were dull and his face was tense. He had been coughing for a few days due to chest congestion and he was also limping.

Dodger lay quietly on the floor as I began to give him healing and I immediately picked up an energy blockage in the left side of his chest area. Dawn confirmed that it was the left heart valves that were damaged. He started panting as the healing energy changes took effect and tried to move away from me. No doubt he associated the tingling sensation with feeling unwell and wondered if it was his heart trouble again. After a while he settled and obviously realised that the feelings he had in his body were OK and that he was not ill this time. Suddenly he sat up and stared at me in a most peculiar way. 'He's going to give you a hug,' said Dawn. 'He does that to people he likes.' Sure enough Dodger reached up with both front paws and placed them onto my shoulders. Then I felt a squeeze around my body as he actually hugged me, nuzzling into my neck with his nose. It was a truly amazing feeling.

Dodger then trotted away and lay down and I resumed the healing treatment as he sighed and then yawned several times. I could see by the faraway look in his eyes that he was responding to the release of endorphins through healing. At the end of the session he seemed much brighter and started to play. I visited again two weeks later and Dawn told me that the day after the healing he was 'acting like a two year old'! He appeared in less discomfort from the arthritis and she had noticed a different expression on his face. He had stopped coughing and was full of energy, running around wanting to play with the other dogs. I noticed that his features did look different; his face looked far less pinched and much softer. He wanted to play with me when I arrived and after a while he jumped up and gave me his trademark hug. It was delightful to see him so happy. Dodger has had several healing sessions and after two years is still with us.

🐾 Healing helps the body to recover from shock due to rebalancing of the energy levels. Healing aims for harmony at all levels.

🐾 Healing can be useful with skin problems because it works on a general level to help the vitality of organs, and assists remedies being given to work on a deeper level.

🐾 It has been shown scientifically that healing can improve the rate of tissue repair and recovery after surgery or illness.

🐾 The symptoms and stress caused by terminal illness can be eased – see Chapter 10.

🐾 Healing has been known to help slow down, or even stop, the rate of tumour growth and is useful when combined with other natural treatments such as homeopathy and acupuncture.

Healing as first aid

In cases of trauma you can give healing as first aid while you are waiting for the vet to arrive or as you are being taken to the clinic. Some sources say that healing should not be given until wounds have been stitched or bones set because it may activate premature repair, but I personally do not agree with this. The universal source of healing energy connects with an individual body to work for its greater good and will know what is best at any particular time. Healing is beneficial for all trauma as it helps the body to combat the effects of shock; it is also comforting. *Remember that for the very ill or traumatised animal you can safely give healing while other treatments and therapies are actually being administered.*

Healing has been proven to stimulate and improve tissue repair, and it certainly helps with shock. However, after an illness or injury the pet may not recover the same level of previous health, but healing aims to strengthen the process to the best possible level. Healing can produce a

Healing doesn't just target specific areas but the whole being of the animal. Treating the whole body at a deep spiritual level has a knock-on effect everywhere and individual problems may resolve themselves.

feeling of inner peace and calm and also helps release pent-up energy, which – if suppressed – may lead to depression due to the stresses surrounding orthodox treatment and recovery. The pet doesn't understand these necessary procedures and can often view them as a form of abuse, so becoming more and more unhappy.

With all forms of life, there comes a time when body cells are too damaged or diseased for the inner resources to be stimulated into recovery by healing and then death may result. Healing given at this time is very beneficial to both pet and care-giver. This is described in more detail in Chapter 7.

4 Communicating with animals through healing

The real voyage of discovery consists not in seeking new lands but in seeing with new eyes.

Marcel Proust

Learning to trust our instincts

Firstly let me explain what I mean by communicating with our pets. Communication is developing our intuition and establishing a rapport on a mind-to-mind level, picking up sensations, thoughts and feelings and then being able to act on that information. True communication is about blending energies with our pets and recognising a common spiritual purpose. This process enhances our lives and helps us to gain insight into who we truly are.

I am horrified to see that there are now gadgets on the market, designed to hang around the neck of a cat or dog, that display words or phrases supposedly informing us what the pet is feeling and thinking. Gadgets are superficial and like all gimmicks open to misuse, but most of all they evade the issue of humans actually establishing their own rapport with other creatures. We have mind energies to do this through our brains – only a small fraction of our mental brain capacity is currently used, so we have far more ability than we actually realise. We just need to expand and develop our capability to tap into who and what we are. Having done that, we can tune into the minds of our animal friends and indeed all of the universal energies. Gadgets do not allow us to expand our abilities and inner resources – only our own efforts encourage this process. Communication with our pets is part of our own spiritual evolution.

Each one of us has the ability to communicate with animals if we open up the energy channels we already possess and which are part of

> Animal communication skills work through the same energy connection as healing – activated by our love and intent. Humans can communicate verbally but animals say a lot more if we listen.

us. Healing and communication are linked and go hand-in-hand because both work with the same vibrations of energy. I have explained in earlier chapters how hands-on healing is more than just making an energy connection to the pet to help with various problems. Healing allows us to make a deep communication connection by receiving information back through our fingertips and into our minds about what is going on within the pet. Even if we don't touch the pet, the information travels to us from the aura – the energy field surrounding all creatures – which carries information about the animal's emotional, mental and physical health. Many times people say to me, 'I know this sounds crazy, but I feel as though my relationship with this animal goes very deep, as though I understand their thoughts and feelings.' To me this isn't crazy but

Healing can be safely given by us to any animal, no matter what age or for what condition. The eyes emit electromagnetic energy and when we connect through healing there is an intensification of this energy – which is life-force energy – through the eyes. The life force carries the soul energy, hence the saying 'the eyes are the window to the soul'. Especially when giving healing, we can look into an animal's eyes and see this powerful spirit looking back at us deep into the heart of our own existence – our own soul energy is revealed. Animals can read our soul energy not just through our eyes, but from our own energy field because the soul energy communicates with all living beings, bringing deep knowledge and understanding; and the healer's love stimulates this.

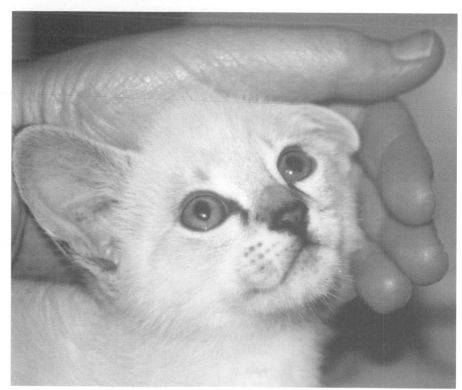

beautiful, for we share a common soul energy and to feel that rapport is very special.

Many people get information from the auras and energy fields of both other people and their pets in what they call 'hunches' or 'intuition'. Sometimes they act on it, and other times they dismiss it, but many times people tell me that their hunches are ultimately proved right. Often they feel overwhelmed by conflicting opinion, including that of professionals, and so don't follow up their communications. One man contacted me about his dog. He had felt for months that the dog was trying to tell him that it had a health problem but the dog seemed really well, going for long walks and eating and drinking normally. It was when the man sat by his dog in the evening with his hand resting on its shoulder that he received these feelings of foreboding. It was only some time after that he realised that he had been tapping in to the aura and healing energy. Suddenly one day the dog collapsed and died. A post mortem showed liver disease, something the dog would have had for several months although for some reason didn't present any obvious symptoms. The man now regrets that he didn't pursue the dog's messages to him for help as blood tests would have highlighted the problem. It is just a matter of us building up the confidence that we *can* communicate with our pets and receive information from them and therefore seek advice accordingly. More and more vets today are open to these things and will listen carefully to the care-giver who feels that something is wrong with their pet even if there are no obvious symptoms.

'Energy follows the direction of thought'

Telepathy

Telepathy is a spiritual discipline that comes naturally to animals because they are very much in tune with nature and the non-physical side to their being – the energy field of life. A great deal of research has shown that animals do have powers of telepathy and perception beyond human understanding. Animals, including birds, fish and insects, have uncanny abilities and senses far beyond those of the human race. They attempt to communicate with the world around them, including us and each other, all the time. Humans are on the whole switched off from receiving these complex and subtle communications and ignore all the silent voices – we are the poorer spiritually for it. Humans struggle to tune in to their telepathic senses (intuition, sixth sense or extra-sensory perception) owing to being out of touch with their true spiritual self. This blocks out sensitivity to the whole spectrum of energy fields and subtle levels of

THE BABY ALPACA

Alfie the baby alpaca was very scared when he saw humans and ran around hiding behind his mother. He was five weeks old but very small for his age. Alfie was underweight at birth and as his mother had insufficient milk he hadn't gained weight properly. Consequently he had been bottle-fed twice a day with milk made for lambs. He was still very weak and the lady who looked after the alpacas was worried that he might not survive when the cold winter weather came.

I held Alfie in my arms to give him healing, and he was smaller than a puppy that I had treated a couple of hours before. I could feel him respond to the healing because he relaxed and leaned on me – then he yawned and shut his eyes. The whole herd slowly gathered round us, then they came up to sniff my hair and watch me intently as I held their baby. Alfie made little grunting, calling noises; the other alpacas in the herd made the same noise and came to gently nuzzle us both as if to say they understood what was going on. Several blew softly over my hands as I gave the healing and I could feel the vibrations of their intense communication to me and to each other.

I kept the time short as I do with most young animals so as not to stress them unduly and because they usually have a short attention span. This doesn't affect the benefits of the healing though – energy travels in a split second into the body. When I let him go, Alfie skipped off to stand behind his mother again. A couple of weeks later I was very pleased to hear that Alfie was gaining weight and getting much stronger, and not long after that he was as big as the other baby alpacas born at the same time as him. The alpacas' love and communication during the healing opened up to me a deeper knowledge and perspective of animals, confirming to me that we should not place one species higher than another.

vibrational information. But this telepathic mental ability is not lost, just shut away inside us – we can start to develop our potential any time that we choose to open the door and explore our hidden depths.

Reasons to get in touch

There are many reasons why people may wish to communicate with animals. With my own work as a healer I concentrate on picking up sensations of emotional and physical imbalance and energy blockages. Another very valid reason for wanting to communicate is to develop a

closer bond with the pet. Other people express a desire to reach a deeper and more mystical level of understanding with their animal. Giving healing helps in all of these areas too, and communication together with healing is a very powerful tool.

There are sadly times when a pet has gone missing and the stricken human wants to send out a lifeline of thought to hopefully help guide it back home. We can, of course, also communicate with our pets after they have died because their signature energy field cannot be destroyed but still exists somewhere on another level in another form of life. Last summer I took a break from my writing one day and went to sit under a tree in the garden with my new kittens. I put my water glass down on the lawn and as I did so saw that next to it lay a cat collar name disc. When I picked it up I noticed that it had belonged to one of my cats who had died 18 months previously. Not only that, the disc was one he had lost in the garden of a house we had lived in several years before. The disc is metal and after all those years outside should have been corroded yet it was unmarked, even looked polished, and my old telephone number was clearly visible on it. It was a communication from my old cat that he was still very much with me and approved of the new kittens.

Receiving communication

Often clients have said to me, 'I wish I could do what you do and pick things up from the animals to help them.' All of us can communicate with our pets, just as each of us can be a healer. Animal communication skills work through the same energy connection as healing – activated by our love and intent. Inside us is all the knowledge we need; we just need to find the key to help us remember what we already know about self, the soul and other realms. A woman contacted me to say she had taken two courses in animal communication, but she still didn't think that she was very good and so she wanted to know how she could improve. I suggested that she take a course in healing, because if we are not in touch

> Love exchanged between ourselves and the animal becomes the communication pathway and a thought of intent becomes the bridge. We are all from the same creative source and part of the same cosmic energy, so once we recognise that we have the ability we can begin to communicate on a soul level.

with the pets' energy field then we will be unable to communicate, no matter how hard we try. I heard from her a while later – her animal communication abilities had taken off after she had developed her healing ability, and needless to say she was very excited about the change.

Giving healing is a two-way communication that opens up a very complex and deep information channel. As well as picking up communication via healing, there are other ways in which we can converse with our pets and they with us. However, many things can block this flow of information from the human's point of view, including stress, family problems, feeling upset, past experiences, poor health, depression, etc. In my experience animals seem able to pick up information from us no matter how they are feeling, which is why healing is so beneficial for them.

There are several ways that information can come to us from our pets during healing, for example from the pet's own energy field to our own energy field as we touch it, or from the mind of the pet direct to our mind as we concentrate on it. Information can include any of the following:

- Hearing words or sentences. These can describe a complete situation or just be a clue for us to work out.
- Mental pictures or visualisations. These can take the form of seeing something happening to the animal, but they can also be as seen through the pet's eyes.
- Knowledge that just seems to appear in your mind, which you then have to put into words. This is intuitive communication and is the way that I often work.
- Sensations within your body reflecting what is happening to the pet. These can be emotional or mental as well as physical sensations. Often when the sensations from the animals are emotional they can cause the healer to feel momentarily tearful. They are, of course, the pet's unshed tears reflected onto the human energy field before discharging.

If you are picking up emotional disturbances, this can assist you to make lifestyle changes to help resolve problems. Depending on the nature of the problem, you may wish to also involve a holistic vet and/or pet behaviour therapist as well as giving some healing treatments yourself. When picking up physical sensations, you may feel drawn to certain areas of the body. If you are concerned you should ask a vet to investigate further.

Exercise: developing animal communication skills

Step 1: choose a quiet time

Choose a time when the pet you wish to communicate with is resting. It is very distracting if you have picked cat play time and it is bouncing around the room, or the dog is barking at the workmen next door, for example. If you have pets other than the one you wish to link with it is OK if they are in the same room as long as they are in resting mode too.

It is essential to have some quiet time first of all to meditate (see page 76). This gets you used to raising the mind onto a higher level and to building mental communication skills. Turn off all the telephones in the house so that you are not disturbed. Animals will be more relaxed when the house is peaceful anyway and it makes it easier to tune into their energies.

Step 2: be at peace

Always select a time when you are as unstressed as possible. It's difficult for many of us to be totally stress-free, but it is better to communicate when rested rather than, say, after a journey home from work, or after a meal (without alcohol) rather than when hungry, and when we feel balanced rather than after an argument.

Step 3: be comfortable

Comfort is essential for both you and your pet so the room must be neither too hot nor too cold. Have a glass of mineral water nearby and writing materials so you can make a note of what happens.

Step 4: ask your pet if it is the right time to communicate with it

How will you know this? The animal may show responses such as a positive body movement (stretching, sighing, eyes closing, licking or generally becoming more peaceful) or you will find yourself suddenly feeling more relaxed with images/words starting to flow into your mind.

Step 5: the communication keys

These are the same as for general healing – an open heart chakra linking with that of the animal and positive thoughts of love offering help. Imagine positive thoughts of love offering help. Imagine that you are being bathed in a warm golden light and that a beam connects you both, joining your souls together through your hearts. The atmosphere around you may feel different as the biomagnetic field charges more strongly and the light intensity in the room may change. The pet or pets should be very relaxed by this stage too.

> ## Our extra-sensory abilities
>
> - When words and pictures are received in the mind it is described as clairvoyance – which means to see clearly.
> - When words are heard this is called clairaudience – to hear clearly.
> - When sensations are felt it is called clairsentience – to feel clearly.
>
> If we receive telepathic information from a person or an animal we are energy receivers and when we send a thought out that they receive we are energy transmitters.

Contact communication

Mentally speak your pet's name so that you establish a mind-to-mind link.

Next place a hand or fingertips very gently over the pet's body. You can either touch softly or keep your hand above the body about an inch away. Move your hand gently, pausing from time to time and allowing your mind to absorb the subtle flow of energies.

Does a word come to you?

Explore the experience – can you hear the word or does it come into your mind as though written down? If so, is it in colour or in black and white? If you speak the words out loud that you have been given, do more follow? You might receive a whole sentence about how the pet is feeling.

Are you getting pictures?

How do they appear? Are they in multi-colour or a single colour? Are they bright or dull? Are the pictures moving like a film or still like a photograph? Is there a time scale to the pictures – do you feel you are in the past or the present?

Are you getting sensations?

Let your mind wander around your own body. Does anything feel different to you suddenly which you interpret could be a sensation coming from the pet? Is there an ache or twinge somewhere in your body, or can you feel heat or tingling? Do you have a sudden awareness of feeling upset, angry, lonely or fearful, which could be emotions coming from the pet? Why do you feel this is so and how can you help?

Non-contact communication

There are times when you cannot touch a pet to communicate or to give healing. However, it is still possible to receive information from the energy field because it radiates out from the body to infinity. Stand as close to the pet as possible and start by allowing your mind to float free and your vision to become soft. Look at the pet's aura (about an inch above the body). This can often be seen as a golden light or a shimmer. Do you sense dark spots or colours in the aura? If so, concentrate on what this means. What words, pictures or impressions come to you to explain this? You may also feel sensations in your body reflected from the pet in the same way as if you were doing contact communication (see page 74).

At the vet's

You may want to communicate with your pet in a veterinary hospital if it is very sick and you feel frustrated that you cannot do more for it. Then tell your pet this and let it know that you are doing everything you can to help with the problem. Pets are very understanding and sympathetic to human emotions so the more upbeat we can try to be the better.

Don't be afraid to tell the pet how much you love it. You can say this out loud or silently from your mind to your pet's mind if you prefer. Love creates an enormous wave of positive healing energy and opens the heart chakra, which in turn helps the patient feel more peaceful and protected.

Receiving the information

When the information starts to come to you from the pet, send a thought back to it, such as, 'How can I help you? What can I change to make your life better? Is something bothering you?' Send thoughts of love with each question and let the pet know that you wish to help it. At these times it's common to feel surrounded by a soft light or to feel that everything seems far away as your energies blend together in love and harmony. This is also a time to give some healing as described in Chapter 7.

Keep the sessions short initially and write everything down, including your feelings and responses from the pet, so that you can refer to this record later on.

Communicating with wild, farm and factory animals

The energy communication abilities of domestic pets and other animals is exactly the same. All life communicates in a variety of complex ways but our pets will develop more sophisticated means as they live in close proximity to human beings. All animals, however, send out energy vibrations of their thoughts and emotions. Wild, farm, factory and laboratory animals are no different to our pets when it comes to thoughts, feelings and emotion.

Millions of animals every year live and die in distress in places that exploit and abuse their sacred life, including factory farms, fur farms, laboratories, circuses, unscrupulous breeding places and many theme parks and poorly run zoos. Surely the least that we can do is to send these pitiful and abused creatures some thoughts of love every day. Each time we make one of these energy connections our aura becomes brighter and lighter as we share and acknowledge the common source of all life. If we wish to be efficient and powerful communicators with our pets we need to expand our consciousness to receive and send healing communication to all life on this planet as often as we possibly can.

Meditation tip

You may find it easier to meditate with others. This creates a pool of strong energy and helps individuals to concentrate. Make sure the people you choose to meditate with are of a like mind and sympathetic to animal healing, otherwise negative atmospheres can be created.

Exercise: a meditation for pet healing

Regular meditation is really important and necessary to strengthen healing potential and the development of our intuitive side. Through meditation we get in touch with our inner selves and contact the soul energy. Like healing, meditation is a living prayer. Your soul is the foundation of your own energy field and the site of your healing connection to the universal mind. The following meditation is designed to help you on your animal healing pathway. It is simple but effective and should ideally be done once a week. Meditation helps not only to develop our healing abilities but also opens our intuitive communication channels.

It is very easy to meditate and there is no mystique to it. Finding the time is the biggest stumbling block in our busy lives, but just half an hour is all that it takes to notice the benefits for your healing work. You may see lights or colours as you meditate; these are sparks of energy connecting you to the healing source in your own healing space.

Sit somewhere that is comfortable for you where you can relax. It can be indoors or outside.

Eliminate disturbances

If you are indoors, switch off and unplug computers or televisions near to you. The electrical charges from them are not helpful during meditation. Switch off the telephones so that you are not disturbed.

Background sounds

If you are indoors, it is helpful to play some suitable meditation or healing music to help relax the mind. A busy mind full of everyday thoughts will not be able to reach the meditative state. If you are going to meditate outdoors, then the natural sounds of wildlife and gentle running water have the same effect as the music.

Body position

Sit with your hands resting in your lap, palms either facing each other or upwards. It is important to take a moment to let all tension in the body go – drop the shoulders, allow the neck to feel loose, feel the legs connect with the earth beneath you and allow your breathing to become deep, slow and rhythmical. Breathe in deeply and slowly and as you breathe out let all feelings of tension flow out with that breath. Do this three times then go on to the next step.

Focus the mind

Choose something natural that you personally find inspiring to focus on as you begin to relax. This might be a flower, a piece of rock, a gemstone or even a candle. Allow your gaze to remain on your chosen object and draw its beauty into your mind. What sort of shapes are there – round, square, oblong, curved? How many colours can you see? What else do you notice? When you have all the information in your mind, close your eyes and visualise the colours that you noticed flowing through your body then outwards from the top of your head into

the universe. You should now be feeling even more relaxed and maybe even a little sleepy.

Experience the inner animal

Now you are ready to go on to the next stage of experience. In your mind's eye, see (envision) an animal of the type that you wish to give healing to, for example a cat, dog, rabbit, etc. Don't focus on a pet you know, but an animal in general. Project your thoughts so that you have the sensation of being inside the animal, be aware of a different body shape and look out at the world through its eyes. Allow your mind to explore the new body sensations and experience. How does it feel to move around on four legs, to have wings instead of arms, to have a tail to express emotion, to be much smaller than humans, not to be able to use words, to be at the beck and call of humans? Allow your mind energy to blend with the mind energy of the animal. What thoughts come to you? What emotions fill your senses? You are now connecting and communicating your mind with the universal mind energy of animals and not only seeing the world, but feeling the world, as they do. This is experiencing the animal consciousness. By repeating this meditation often you will become much more intuitive in your healing work with animals.

Healing thoughts

End your meditation by opening your heart chakra as wide as possible to let your love pour out to all animals in need. To do this, place your hand on your chest and then take it slowly away. As you do so, envision that you are drawing out from your heart a golden beam of light. With your love send this beam out into the universe to reach every animal that needs help.

Unwind

Relax and chill out now – take a deep breath, stretch out with your arms above your head then open your eyes. Drink a glass of mineral water. You should now be feeling very peaceful and new knowledge will be with you. You are now on your journey of developing your animal healing and skills.

Practise as much as you can in order to become a strong healer. Once you have become confident in giving healing and have got used to applying your mind to it, you will find that you can offer healing anywhere if the situation arises. Even a busy noisy environment will not be off-putting to you when an animal is in need.

BILLIE'S EPILEPSY

Billie was ten years old when I first started giving him healing. He was a Staffordshire bull terrier, and a very large, stocky one at that. However, Billie was as gentle a dog as you can get and lived in a house with another dog of the same breed, Dixie. Billie was one of the many epileptic dogs I've treated with healing and he had been having fits for seven years and was on both conventional and homeopathic medication. Billie seemed very low in himself when I first met him and I noted that he also suffered from arthritis. His family had considered whether or not it was time to put him to sleep, as his epilepsy was now so severe.

Billie was very unsure of the healing sensations during the first treatment and kept moving around, panting quite a bit, and giving me puzzled looks. After a while he settled and lay down beside me and at the end his eyes looked brighter and his care-giver noticed that his body shape appeared 'lifted'.

I was pleased to hear that there was a rapid and real improvement in Billie after a couple of sessions of healing. Over the months Billie came to really love the healing and he used to fall into a deep sleep and snore loudly, and often he wouldn't even wake up to say goodbye when I left. His friend Dixie also decided that healing was definitely her cup of tea. During Billie's first session she edged closer to me, eventually leaning against my legs. She then closed her eyes and was quite clearly enjoying the beneficial effects of the healing energy. After that time Dixie would always join us and share the healing, which she also needed because she had kidney problems. Barbara's two-year-old son would also often watch and point to areas on Billie's body during the healing. 'I can tell the healing is communicating to him where Billie is hurting,' Barbara would tell me. Children are frequently very receptive to healing energies even at a very young age so this was no surprise to me.

As time went on Billie began to respond very well to the strengthening and rebalancing of the healing. Healing can help homeopathic remedies work better too. His fits became less frequent and when they occurred he recovered from them much more quickly. Within a couple of weeks of his first healing treatment, his care-givers noticed a big improvement in Billie's enjoyment of life and his sense of well-being. In fact, he did so well that he started going for long walks again and the conventional medication dosage was able to be reduced. The vet said to Barbara, 'Whatever you are doing for Billie, carry on with it because it's working.'

One very sad day I received a phone call to say that Dixie had passed away from kidney failure. On this occasion I gave Billie healing for his grief over the loss of his best friend. Several months later, I placed my hands on to Billie to

start the healing and was concerned to notice that his energy field felt very sluggish and irregular. In my experience, this means that something is either wrong or about to become wrong. Billie communicated to me a problem around his stomach area and I asked Barbara if Billie had gone off his food or had been sick. He had not; indeed the dog loved his food so much that he had a waistline problem! I suggested that Barbara took Billie to the vet for check-up, which she did that same day. He could find nothing in particular, but noticed that the dog was unhappy, so he increased the medication to help with pain relief. A month later when I saw Billie again, the depletion in energy I could pick up was more marked. Two weeks later Billie collapsed and when he was taken to the clinic, the vet found a lump. Billie was diagnosed as having stomach cancer and was very ill, and the kindest thing was to put him to sleep. Billie was cremated and his ashes were scattered next to Dixie's in the local park at a favourite spot where they played together. His family felt satisfied that they had done everything they possibly could for him. I still have in my study a photo of Billie in a Christmas hat, which was sent to me the month before he died.

5 Healing and the human link

> Within this sphere of heartfelt listening and sharing lies the soul of true communion with the animal nations – a deep and nurturing affection that can, I believe, restore our spirits and heal our earth.
>
> Susan Chernak McElroy, from *Animals as Teachers and Healers*

Pets are good for us

Keeping pets is good for us. They can act as our healers and can even be good for our health. Numerous studies have shown that cuddling or stroking a pet can lower blood pressure and has a positive effect on mood and well-being. The University of New York carried out an experiment with 240 married couples and gave them a stressful task to do. Some of those being studied had a friend with them and others a pet. The blood pressure of those who had a pet with them while they completed the task was lower than those who were with a friend. Scientists say that this is yet more proof that having a pet is good for our health as stress lowers the immune system. Another study demonstrated that keeping a pet reduces cholesterol levels and for these reasons pet owners may be less prone to heart attacks than non pet owners. Sick people who have contact with pets are known to benefit and stress-related blood pressure can be reduced by half. Researchers in the US have also found that pet owners make on average ten per cent fewer visits to the doctor. Expressing our feelings boosts the immune system and improves our health, and pets can help us to express our emotions. Giving a pet healing helps it to express emotional energy so both human and pet benefit in this way.

Pets provide invaluable companionship and help people to make friends. For the elderly, pets can lessen feelings of loneliness by giving them a purpose in life. However, it's not just furry creatures that benefit our health. Watching fish in an aquarium has been found to reduce anxiety levels at the dentist's as much as having hypnosis. In our two-way relationship pets are very much tuned in to our energies and dogs are now even being trained to detect when a person is about to have an

epileptic seizure. Pets give us their love in return for our love, although it can be an uneasy relationship sometimes with many problems. I hope that hands-on healing, by taking you on to another level of understanding with your pet, will help you to have a more meaningful relationship together.

- Giving healing to our pets is a two-way relationship. Healing connects us with the animal's soul and also allows us to reach deep into our own soul. Pets help us along our spiritual pathway, even if we do not believe in such things, because when we have loved and cared for an animal we are changed for the better. Even the pain of losing a pet teaches us the ultimate lesson – that being loved and giving love creates a bond that can never be broken.

- Animals have souls just as humans do. The soul is part of the life force energy that exists in all living beings. The soul links with the body and mind, and connects to the universal energy source. On a day-to-day level, the soul operates and expresses through the personality. Spiritual healing reaches all these aspects of the individual. The soul level, the deepest part of the life-force energy, is where true healing begins. Many great minds through history have recognised this, as do more and more animal healthcare professionals today. The Greek philosopher Hippocrates said, 'The soul is the same for all living creatures although the body of each is different,' while Pythagoras commented, 'Animals share with us the privilege of having a soul.' Denying that animals have souls gives an excuse for lack of respect for other forms of life. Even if you don't agree with the concept of animals having souls, the healing you give will still work on whatever level is possible. Our love is the most important requirement to make the healing connection.

- It is important to always remember that we never 'own' an animal, we are their companions, their care-givers, their healers. We can never own another soul, whether it be human or animal.

Pets as healers

There are many times when pets give us healing when we are in need, upset, lonely, sad or unwell. It is good to touch them over the brachial major 'key' chakra so that the powerful exchange of healing energy, allowing light to enter both souls, benefits both of you. At this time

We need another and a wiser and perhaps a more mythical concept of animals.... We patronise them for their incompleteness, for their tragic fate of having taken form so far below ourselves. And therein we err and greatly err. For the animal shall not be measured by man. In a world older and more complete than ours, they move finished and complete, gifted with extensions of the senses we have lost or never attained, living by voices we shall never hear. They are not brethren; they are other nations, caught with ourselves in the net of life and time, fellow prisoners of the splendour and travail of the earth.

Henry Beston (an American author, 1888–1968),
The Outermost House

animal and human are as one; both are healers, both receivers and givers. The energy field of both human and animal rebalances as the healing energy flows from one to the other until there is a golden glow around them. This is a very special time – very beautiful and precious. People ask me if we drain the animal's energy at these times. I don't believe we do, as long as we do not ask it of our pets constantly. They have an abundance of love to give, and they attach no condition to it; they just want to love us. Love is the key to successful healing and animals have lots of love. However, if we are at a stage in our lives where we need a lot of healing, then it is better to seek professional help before we swamp our pet with our disturbed energy. Humans can reflect their problems onto pets, unsettling their own energy, and this can manifest as health problems in them. At these times both pet and person can feel the benefit of healing from an outside and neutral source.

Animals choose us

We are part of the natural order of this world and what we do to even the tiniest creature affects our own energy field. We can add to the world's darkness or its light by our thoughts and deeds, and of course our own energy field responds accordingly. I believe that we are not complete until we have loved an animal and shared our life with it because our soul energy is linked to the energy of animals. I further believe that we will remain unfulfilled unless we experience this relationship. The love for an animal awakens our soul fully and therefore we grow spiritually from the experience. What we gain from this love

SANTA

Santa is blonde and gorgeous, a large golden retriever. When I first met him he was six years old and his vet had asked me to give him healing because over a two-year period he'd had eleven malignant skin tumours removed. When I put my hands on to Santa I felt that he was carrying a great deal of sadness. After a few minutes of giving him healing, it seemed as though our minds became as one. I was taken back to when he was younger and I knew that he had felt unhappy at being a kennel dog. I could pick up his emotions, sense his thoughts, *become* him. Now that I was inside his mind I could tell that he was unfulfilled in his earlier life. Santa is a very clingy and sensitive dog and he wanted to be with people constantly, taking part in family life in order to feel more secure.

I asked his care-giver, Joyce, how long she'd had Santa and where he came from. Everything I was picking up made sense when she told me that Santa had only been with her family for about two years. Before that he had lived in a kennel at the breeders with around 20 other dogs. Although Santa was fed regularly and let out to play with the other dogs each day, he lacked the contact and stimulation that, for him, only living in a home with humans could bring. Although dogs are pack animals, selective breeding over thousands of years has resulted in each breed having individual traits. Labrador retrievers are particularly renowned for being people-orientated, thriving on human attention and company. Santa is just such a dog. Joyce had approached the breeder one day because she wanted a companion for her other dog, also a golden retriever. Santa had been offered to her because the breeder recognised that the dog would be happier living with a family who could offer him the attention he particularly needed. Santa really landed on his paws here because Joyce and her family are exceptional animal-lovers and he now had everything that he ever wanted, including lots of love and fun.

Santa just loved the healing, but at first I could see that he was fighting the sensations that it gave him. His big brown eyes would flicker and shut, then he would open them again as if he didn't want to miss anything. After a while, however, he became very sleepy and with a big sigh lay down onto his side. I was to visit Santa regularly over the next few months and he got to know when I was coming, even though I arrived at different times and on different days. He would go into the room where I gave him healing and flop down, obviously waiting for it with great pleasure. I was thrilled when he started to improve, and over the past three years the tumour rate has slowed right down. Santa has become a real friend and these days is a very happy dog, looking even more gorgeous than ever.

can never be taken away; it is ours for all eternity. Pain and loss are part of this love and will follow the joy and the pleasure as surely as night follows day.

Animals are part of our healing life and frequently choose to be with us to help as guides along life's pathway, or recognise from our aura that we are someone that they would like to be with. We may be guided towards one particular animal, having thought we wanted something else. So many times clients have said to me, 'I don't know why I chose this cat/dog/bunny/bird, etc, because it wasn't what I was looking for.' It was because the animal chose them and the person subconsciously picked up the signals that said, 'I recognise you as someone I want to be with.' The person responded by taking the animal home with them, even though they didn't consciously know why. This has happened to me on several occasions and it was only later when the relationship developed that I realised what I was learning from it; healing is always part of that two-way process.

'Healing is a journey of spiritual communication between you and your pet'

Healing lessons

Animals are part of our life and we need to live alongside them rather than wanting to control or dominate them for they have important things to teach us about ourselves. Healing is a two-way relationship and without our pets we would not develop into the people that we are. We are guided to learn in this life through the form that we are most receptive to and for a lot of people their teachers are animals. We are influenced by our relationships with them and when things go wrong we travel new pathways in the search to help them. By linking to other species as healers, we receive spiritual lessons and strengths. I have learnt that animals have very powerful lessons to bring us. Here are some of the special things that I believe different species can teach us.

- Dogs teach us service and devotion to others.
- Cats teach us independence of spirit and not being afraid to follow our destiny.
- Birds teach us to allow our soul to fly free and expand.
- Small furry creatures teach us to explore the depths of our soul.
- Fish teach us that energy flows without boundaries throughout the universe.
- Reptiles teach us to protect ourselves from negative influences.
- Horses teach us to feel and get in touch with who we truly are.

The sum total of knowledge that animals teach us is to explore ourselves spiritually. However, we humans may not always be listening to the healing lessons being offered, for example:

- If we abuse and neglect dogs, then we will not be exploring the depths of our potential love.
- If we have no empathy or rapport with a cat's natural needs of expression, then we show our fear of our own inner growth.
- If we cage a bird permanently, we are restricting and stunting our own soul development.
- If we keep small furry creatures in small cages rather than in large areas, thus preventing them from running and exploring, then there is little depth to the understanding of our actions.
- If we put fish into an unsuitable and too small environment, we limit the extent of our potential energy strength.
- If we keep reptiles in unnatural conditions then we are open to negative influences.
- If we do not develop a partnership with the horse but seek to dominate it and manipulate its life, then we have no feelings other than on a purely physical level.

Healers of the future

I am frequently heartened when I give healing to animals and children are watching. They appear so aware of natural forces and in tune with energy; and it was, of course, as a child that I started to sense healing energy.

At a meeting I attended, a vet talked about his work with animals in developing countries. The children – between six and twelve years of age – had been encouraged to draw animals as part of an animal welfare education programme and these pictures amazed him. They drew the animals with colours around them in unusual shapes and when the vet asked them why, they explained that the colours meant what was wrong either physically or emotionally. I was able to further enlighten the vet that these children were seeing the colours of the animals' auras. This was such a completely natural thing for them to sense that they put it in their pictures.

Time and again children and young people describe seeing colours around my hands when I am giving healing to the family pets, and talk about sensations in their bodies too – 'It's like fairy dust twinkling in my

FOUR TERRITORIAL BOYS

Julie shares her cottage with four male oriental cats – two sets of brothers. Oriental cats can be quite a handful as they have big personalities and are very vocal – just the type of cat I personally adore! As time went by and these boys got older, they started having serious territory and dominance disputes. The end result was that three of them, Rupert, Ossie and Joshua, although neutered, had started spraying extensively round the house. Julie's home is a beautiful modern example of feng shui design with white and cream décor and the cats were having a field day making the furniture very wet, and very smelly, with their constant spraying. Julie was having to place tin foil around all the walls to protect the paintwork and furniture, and apart from looking ugly, it was very stressful for her.

The cats were eventually referred to me by homeopathic vet Cheryl Sears who felt that healing could help release the emotional blockages causing much of the problems. The first cat I treated was Rupert, as he was the most angry and spraying out of control around the whole house. Rupert was a little reluctant to sit on my lap during the first visit, but he eventually settled down, gave a big sigh and fell asleep. I felt his body become very warm under the areas where my hands passed and Julie noticed this too. When he got down on to the floor after the session ended, Rupert appeared quite unsteady for a few seconds and he sat down to gather his thoughts by a sunny window. Ossie came by presently and instead of getting aggressive, Rupert rubbed noses with him. It was an encouraging start.

I visited again two weeks later and Julie was thrilled to be able to tell me that Rupert had become much more sociable with all the other cats and was spraying less. After the third healing treatment he stopped spraying completely and is obviously a much more laid back cat – so much so he is putting on rather too much weight now! I then proceeded to offer healing to Joshua and Ossie too. After about 20 minutes, when I had finished, Julie said, 'He looks completely different already. His eyes look softer and his coat is like silk.' Normally a cat to run off and hide, Joshua sat calmly by me and proceeded to have a wash.

Ossie was always very unhappy with strangers, so I gave him healing while he sat on Julie's lap. He was quite suspicious of what I was doing and kept a wary eye on my fingers as I lightly touched him. Julie felt a lot of tingling and warmth in her hands as she was holding him while I was directing healing to him. He too appeared very calm and relaxed at the end of the session and Julie later reported that Ossie was happier and more confident when visitors came to the house. Instead of leaving the room when someone calls by, now he stays and allows himself to be touched. Julie also noticed that he is less frenetic about life and is in general happier in his own space. All four cats get on much better together now and, very importantly from Julie's point of view, she has a cleaner and sweeter-smelling house!

hands. . . there is a weird feeling in my fingers. . . .' Children can also pick up on the deep communication aspect from the energy field and tell me how the pet is feeling from sensations that come to them as I give healing.

It is good to encourage children to be healers for the future of our world. It's a well documented fact that serial killers first practise by torturing and killing animals, and animal abusers usually go on to harming humans. As St Francis of Assisi, the patron saint of animals, so aptly put it, 'If you have men who will exclude any of God's creatures from the shelter of compassion and pity, you will have men who will deal likewise with their fellow men.' To teach children to use their hands for healing, not hurting, is therefore a very positive thing to do.

6 Animal chakras

Every part of this earth is sacred, because everything is connected, like the blood which unites one body.

Native American Indian saying

The main function of the chakras is to transmit and absorb energies and thus form a link between the vital life force energy and every cell of the physical body. One of the things that I tell people when I am giving talks or demonstrations on animal healing is that there is nothing 'New Age' about chakras. There has been much written about them in the past few years due to growing interest in natural therapies and energy medicine, so many people mistakenly think that they are a recent idea or an unproven phenomenon. That is not so, however! Chakras can be measured with scientific instruments and have been demonstrated to be

Chakras are funnel-shaped centres of energy. They flow in both clockwise and anticlockwise directions and can be felt by placing the hands over the body. In good health they have strong energy and where there is a problem, either mentally, emotionally or physically, the flow becomes weak.

areas of the body where the energy is at its maximum concentration. This is something that our ancestors understood several thousand years ago; in fact, the word chakra comes from an ancient Sanskrit word meaning wheel.

Chakras regulate the flow of energy through the body's energy system, including that of our companion animals. Energy flows through the chakras in a circular way, moving both clockwise and anti-clockwise. However, they are not circular in shape but are more like a flower with several symmetrical petals. These 'petals' intertwine like fingers as the chakra revolves. Chakras also have a positive and a negative polarity, which means that they pull in two opposing directions.

Animal chakras and human chakras

Humans have seven major chakras, with numerous minor ones linked to them. All animals have chakras, but a while back I made an interesting discovery – that animals have an extra major chakra, the brachial chakra or 'key' chakra (see page 101). The seven main chakras corresponding to those of humans are situated along the spine. They are found in everything that has a spine, which means all animals, birds and fish. When I place my hands onto an animal and pick up the chakra flow, I am able to both see and feel the concentrations of energy. If I can sense the energy going anti-clockwise I know that the healing is having an effect, but that the chakra is unbalanced. When I can feel the energy flowing through the chakra in a clockwise direction I feel very pleased because then I know that the animal's body is rebalancing. There comes a point when the clockwise flow stops and then I know that the chakra has stabilised.

In general, animal chakras are considerably bigger in relation to their bodies than human chakras. Also animal chakras have a more active oscillation and stronger cycling of energy. The resistance, i.e. the 'push' away to the hand, also appears more powerful than in humans when the chakra is rebalanced. This is partly due to the fact that human lifestyles tend to keep our energy systems running low most of the time. Some of the cause is environmental, such as the way we live, the polluted food we eat, the chemicals in our home and workplace stress, but mainly it is caused by how we think and view life and our existence. Stress, striving for material possessions, relationship difficulties, lack of spiritual understanding and neglect of self-nurturing all deplete our chakras and energy systems in general. We need to surround ourselves with good

energy and people of a like mind, and make sure we are not contributing to the damage of our world with our lifestyle. It is good to have regular healing ourselves, or even other forms of natural therapies to rebalance and boost our healing potential.

Animals are far simpler than humans in their requirements for life. They ask for food, water, shelter, companionship and freedom. An animal doesn't care what their human friends look like, how they wear their hair, what age they are or what clothes they have on. Neither do animals care whether the furniture, car or house is new or fashionable. They judge us for the brightness of our souls and who we really are inside. That is why their chakras are bigger, brighter and more powerful than ours. Animals are also much more direct about what they want and need from the healing. They are simplistic and undemanding in their approach and in my experience usually ready to let go and move on as much as possible when given healing.

When I run my courses for healers and animal healthcare professionals, students who have had real difficulty working with human chakras are amazed that they can feel them on animals. With practice, it is easier to feel chakra movements on animals than on people, including clockwise and anti-clockwise rotation, vibrations, vertical or horizontal changes, spinning and unwinding. So don't be surprised when you come to give your pet or pets healing if you feel these big powerful centres of energy!

Feeling your pet's chakras

In Chapter 2 I explained about the layers of vibrating electromagnetic energies in the aura that surrounds the body of both humans and animals. Each of these layers is connected to a chakra and it is possible to feel them. Place your hand slightly above your pet's body where the chakra points are (see illustrations on pages 105, 110, 113 and 115). You should be able to feel a resistance of energy, as if your hand is being slightly pushed away. Often a sensation of heat can also be felt in the palm of your hand. With small animals and birds, the sensations will be more subtle and difficult to feel as the energy of the chakras is much closer together. With small animals, I recommend using a fingertip to feel the chakra energy. People familiar with yoga and other forms of meditation will have experienced working through their own chakra energy centres and you can also practise feeling the chakra energy centres on your friends and family.

Chapter 7 explains all the sensations, responses and feelings both you and your pet may experience as you link together during healing, including when you are working with the chakra system, and how you can also give healing by the intuitive 'whole body scan' method.

In a healthy pet (and very importantly the pet needs to be healthy emotionally as well as physically), the 'petals' of the chakras are open and the energy flows freely through them. Where there is imbalance in a pet's body, the chakra becomes blocked and the energy does not flow freely. Often the chakras get so blocked that they shut down. This is not good for the pet's well-being and is a reason why we should regularly channel healing over the chakras to open and clear them, helping to create physical, mental and emotional harmony. By treating each chakra you can give a full healing treatment.

Chakra meditation

It is very important to keep your own chakra system clear when giving healing to a pet as chakras drive your spiritual powers. The chakras store information on everything that goes on in a body, including your pet's, on a spiritual, emotional, mental and physical level. It is our spiritual powers that we call upon when we give healing, so I recommend that the following chakra meditation is carried out for a few minutes before giving healing to a pet – unless, of course, the healing is needed urgently. It is good to do this chakra meditation once a week anyway to help you to be in balance, which in turn will improve your healing connection. Chakra meditation helps to clear the mind and clears energy junk from the body.

This meditation energises and boosts the chakras and makes use of the colour linked to each one. Each of these colours has its own energy wavelength.

Sit quietly in a comfortable chair. Make sure that distractions such as radios, televisions and phones are switched off. Do not cross your arms or legs, and place your hands in your lap. Close your eyes, then visualise in turn the colours of the chakras as follows.

 Violet – the crown chakra at the top of your head
Imagine a large bright purple flower opening upwards from the top of your head.

- Indigo – the brow chakra in the middle of your forehead
  Visualise a deep, midnight blue circle just above your eyes.

- Blue – the throat chakra in the centre of your throat
  Allow your throat and neck to feel bathed in pale blue light.

- Green – the heart chakra in the middle of your chest
  It is very important for your healing that this chakra is fully open. Visualise a huge bright green heart shape covering the whole of your chest area.

- Yellow – the solar plexus chakra across the abdomen
  Imagine that your stomach area is bathed in warm soft yellow sunshine that then flows through your whole body.

- Orange – the sacral chakra across your hips
  Feel the warmth of an orange glow across your hips and lower back that then flows down into your legs.

- Red – the base chakra. You are sitting on this one!
  Visualise a long red tail growing down from the end of your spine and connecting into the earth like a root.

Take your time and hold each colour in your mind for a couple of minutes. If you find it difficult to visualise things, then make yourself a set of coloured cards with the chakra names on and look at each one before you close your eyes to meditate on the particular colour. You should feel very peaceful at the end of this meditation. This technique is great for de-stressing too.

Giving healing over pets' chakras

It is a good idea to practise chakra healing first on a human as they will sit still for you, unlike a more fidgety animal. Ask someone who is sympathetic to what you are doing to sit in a chair so that you can stand behind them. Close your eyes and allow yourself to feel peaceful. Imagine that you are looking at a golden ball of light. When you have this image firmly in your mind, open your eyes and place a hand over the top of the person's head about twelve inches away. Slowly move it down until you feel a resistance. Some people feel heat in the palm or tingling sensations in the fingers. Then move on to the forehead and repeat the exercise, and afterwards to the upper part of the sitter's back where the

93

HONEY'S TAIL GETS BETTER

I was having a cup of fresh peppermint tea in the kitchen of a lovely old farmhouse discussing the horse that I had just treated with his rider. It was a beautiful late autumn day and the weak sun filtered through the shutters and into the room. It was warm in the kitchen because of the Aga oven and lying in a basket in front of it were two tabby cats. They were making the most of the warmth, pressing themselves against the oven, every now and again lazily changing position and stretching out a leg this way and that.

It was during one of these position changes that I noticed that one of the cats had a short tail and a wound at the top of it. Her care-giver explained that the cat was called Honey, was four years old and had been hit by a car the year before. The tail had been broken and as a result the vet had amputated the end of it. There was some nerve damage to the tail and the cat was obviously bothered by the sensations from it for she would lick at the top of her tail until it became raw, which was the wound that I could see.

This was the third time that Honey had caused a wound to appear. On the last two occasions the soreness had lasted for three months and the licking had become so intensive and the wound so large that the vet had fitted a collar around the cat's neck for a while. This new wound had just started to appear and the vet was concerned. As I looked at Honey, I could see that the energy of her base chakra was very weak, which didn't surprise me as any damage to an animal's tail will particularly affect this chakra. I sat down by Honey as she snuggled up to her sister Sugar in the basket and placed my hand just above the sore area. For a couple of minutes Honey carried on snoozing – then, as I felt heat build up under my hand which I held over Honey's base chakra, she opened her eyes and looked round at her back, as if to say, 'What's going on there?' She sniffed the air too, a sure sign that she thought that I was holding something to cause the heat that she could now feel. I gradually felt the heat turn into a beautiful warmth as the energy revitalised. Then she settled down again, little flickers (kinetic energy releases) travelling along her lower back.

I saw Honey again after a month. Her fur had completely re-grown and there was no sign that she'd ever had a problem. I was pleased to hear that within hours of the healing Honey had improved and had stopped licking the area. By the time she visited the vet again a few days later the soreness had gone and he said that no further treatment was necessary.

heart chakra is. Be patient because the sensations are very subtle and it really does require you to have an open and accepting mind. Allow yourself to work intuitively – does your hand want to move forward or back, or from side to side? Work slowly and gently, going with the flow of energy. Keep the experience short, 15 to 20 minutes in total. Now you are ready to start giving healing through your pet's chakras.

Where to begin

The starting position is going to vary, depending on the type of pet and its personality. Some people say that healing should begin with the base chakra, but in my experience the best place to start is the brachial major or 'key' chakra, which is found just in front of and over the shoulder area. Sometimes we may choose to start with another chakra, however. We can listen to our inner healing voice and allow ourselves to be guided by our intuition as to where to place the hands. This is when we are truly listening to and connecting with the energy field of our pets.

Position yourself so that you are facing the animal's side or back. In this way your hand will not appear threatening. If the pet is small, I find it better to use a finger or two instead of the whole hand. Sometimes the subject of your healing may be in a cage, in which case you should point your fingers in the direction of the chakras. Sometimes I rest my fingertips on the side of the cage; other times I stand back, depending on the situation.

Make very gentle contact to begin the healing and if the patient is nervous you can keep your hand a few inches away from the body. After you have felt the flow of healing energy, move your hand to the heart chakra, then down to the solar plexus and sacral chakras, and finally the base chakra. If at any point the pet becomes anxious, stop and touch somewhere else. Hands-on healing is not something that should ever be forced onto any animal; the animal must always be respected if it chooses to move away for any reason. This doesn't mean that the healing has not been effective – it only takes a few seconds to effect the beneficial changes. Experiment with how you like to work when giving the healing. Perhaps you prefer to touch gently or to have your hand above the pet. Either method will work and you may even find that with different pets and in different situations you will wish to give the healing in a different way. This is because you are now working intuitively and listening to the messages from the individual you are helping.

Chakra tip ✓

In larger animals, such as dogs, cats and rabbits, the individual chakra points can easily be found. In the smaller animals and birds this is more difficult so simply direct healing to any area that you can. This will reach the whole body on all levels in the same way as giving healing through the chakras.

What you may feel

It takes time and practice to develop sufficient sensitivity to feel the healing energy through the hands, and the powerful chakra movements. You may feel more over one chakra than another, depending on where the blockages are and how the body is responding. There may be sensations of heat or tingling, or your hand may feel heavy or as though it is being drawn into the pet's body. If it seems that your hand being pushed upwards away from the body, that particular chakra has rebalanced and you can move onto another.

Don't be despondent if you detect very little at first, or nothing at all – the sensations are subtle and some people feel them more quickly than others. It takes time to adjust to a new way of feeling and many healers take years to fully develop their skills and sensitivity. Be patient! As with everything, practice makes for a stronger response and the more you give healing through the chakras, the more sensations you may be able to pick up. You should find it very rewarding to work with your pet in this way and over a period of time begin to notice the benefits and improvements to your pet's general well-being. Healing can be given in this way every week or every few hours for a sick or injured pet.

Chakra healing as first aid

You may be in a situation where first aid healing is needed to help your pet before it can receive veterinary attention. Chakra healing can be given as first aid and I have found this very effective. First aid healing can also be given to injured or traumatised wild animals and birds. If your pet is in shock, has just been injured or has a sudden health problem, place your hand or a fingertip gently above the brachial or 'key' chakra until the vet arrives or until you can get to the clinic. If the shoulder area is injured, give the healing over the sacral chakra. If the animal is in a carrier, direct healing through it as shown in Chapter 7

The hands can be spread over several chakras as pets' bodies are relatively small. In this photograph, three chakras are being covered – the left hand is over both the base chakra (with the fingers) and the sacral chakra (with the bottom of the hand). The right hand is over the solar plexus chakra.

This is a good position to give healing to animals, as most will accept the hands in these areas. It is an especially helpful area in which to give healing for back, hip and hind limb problems, and for liver, kidney, intestine, stomach and reproductive conditions. For animals that don't like being touched in the head area, but which have head/neck problems, healing can be directed up to the head from the sacral chakra.

97

on page 121. Focus with your mind on helping the pet through this stressful time and concentrate on sending thoughts of love and calm. When giving first aid healing, you may feel an unusual pulsing sensation under your hand or fingers as the disturbed energy resonates out of rhythm. After a while you should feel the sensation begin to settle as the healing takes effect.

Affirmations

I have included some affirmations with each chakra description. Affirmations are words or phrases that help us to focus our minds. These simple but powerful statements can have a powerful effect on our mind and well-being. This means that they can help raise our consciousness to a much higher level. Affirmations are a powerful tool aimed at opening up the heart chakra, through which we give healing.

Affirmations are words of compassion and love. They link our mind with our spiritual self, which creates another essential energy process – the *intent* to help and heal. This strong combination of intent and focus links the healing energy to your pet on all possible levels.

Of course the affirmations I have included on the following pages are only my suggestions, ones which work well for me. You can use your own words, and not just with chakra healing, but when giving healing in general. The simplest of words or phrases can be used. For example, saying, 'I love you very much' to your pet has a very powerful energy pattern and will raise both your vibrations considerably. Words of love and good intent link you in a positive way to your pet and help strengthen your healing. Most important is to really and truly mean what you are saying and to keep the affirmations on a spiritual level. Don't ask anything of the pet – just give without any conditions attached.

Colours, planets, body systems and the chakras

Chakras are a map of consciousness within the body, and they are also used to explain the energy currents. When I was developing as a healer we always began and finished our classes by concentrating on the chakras and their relevant colours to strengthen our healing potential. Historically it's accepted that there are seven major chakras situated along the length of the human body. Both Eastern and Western traditions

acknowledge that there are many more minor chakras. Each chakra has a colour, planet and body part or system associated with it.

Colours

The rainbow

Seven of the major chakras have colours that make up the rainbow – red, orange, yellow, green, blue, indigo and violet. Sometimes these pure colours can be sensed or seen over a chakra, but you may in fact sense any colour as the flow of energy is constantly changing. The colours give information about the health, well-being and emotional state of the human or animal. Colour is a language and the chakra system communicates through both energy and colour to relay everything that is happening in a body.

Black for transformation and light

I mentioned earlier my discovery of an eighth major chakra in animals, which I describe for the first time in my book *Healing for Horses*. I have called it the brachial or 'key' chakra because it is the strongest centre of energy and it links to, and activates, all the other chakras. When I discovered it, I knew that it would be associated with a colour as well as a planet and parts of the animal's body. I knew that this 'key' chakra was a very powerful centre of energy and through it you could give healing to the whole body on all levels. By directing healing through this chakra, it is possible to get a very powerful emotional release too.

I puzzled for a while over the colour of this discovery and consulted a friend who is a highly qualified astrologer. Having explained all the qualities of my new discovery, we realised that it was associated with Pluto. Pluto has a powerful influence, causing change to and intensifying the powers of the other planets that its position relates to. It is also the planet of transformation; this can either be symbolic or the actual end of an episode or even physical life. Something has always changed after Pluto's transit and nothing is ever the same again. That planetary link explains this chakra's very spiritual role in releasing and rebalancing emotion, and also its link to the other chakras. In astrological terms, black is associated with Pluto, as the transformation is from darkness to light. Therefore that is the colour I have allocated to this chakra. By giving healing through it we connect a light wavelength, bringing a whole spectrum of beneficial changes.

Some time after the publication of *Healing for Horses*, in which I talk for the first time about this chakra, I met John Cross at a conference.

'Healing aims to convert areas of discord and chaos to harmony and balance'

99

John is the author of several books and an expert on chakras and meridians, and he has a doctorate in acupuncture. He wrote to me after reading my book to query my assumptions. He wondered if the area I had identified was in fact equivalent to the minor shoulder chakra in humans. This is used in the release of toxins and tension, as well as generally 'letting go' and expressing thoughts. Those characteristics seemed indeed to fit the responses I was getting from the brachial major 'key' animal chakra, but I knew without a doubt that this chakra influenced directly all the other major chakras as a catalyst and activated specifically the heart and solar plexus chakras. A few months later John contacted me again. 'Yes, I've felt your chakra for myself now,' he said. John went on to explain that he had been giving healing to a dog and used the occasion to feel for the chakra patterns and their positions. And there it was, just as I explained – the brachial major 'key' chakra!

Black as the healing key

Since then I have researched black as a colour. My explanation for linking it to the brachial major or 'key' chakra is as follows. Imagine that you are lost on a very dark night and cannot see anything. You look this way and that, becoming ever more distressed and hoping that someone will find you. You start to panic at the loss of energy and then become depressed. Suddenly you see a light; someone is shining a torch in your direction. How your heart soars! You feel joy that someone has heard you and has come to show you the way home.

This is what happens when we touch an animal on this chakra. We have heard the cry for help – and it may be emotional, mental or physical – and we are offering light to help them. Why don't humans have this chakra? I believe it is because we are able to be masters of our own personal destiny. Other species tend not to have our choices or our intellect and are at the mercy of humans regarding their lives and habitat. They surely do need our help as we can see from the destruction and cruelty in this world. I believe that this chakra on species other than humans is the key to our relationship with them. It is a spiritual link between us. The important question is what can we learn from animals? Accepting the simplicity of a healing question is often a lesson in itself and our healing touch gives us the answer.

At the heart of blackness or darkness there is always light and it is the light of our own soul – *because we have focused our intent on giving healing* – that illuminates the life force, or soul, of our pets. For them, people who care are indeed 'the light at the end of the tunnel'. This is why I believe that hands-on healing is so successful.

Planets and elements

The planets and elements that relate to each chakra vary according to different sources, so I've included here the ones that I have been most familiar with during my healing career. These planets and elements have qualities and natural energies that are compatible with the pattern of the chakra with which they are connected. There are the well-known elements of earth, fire, water and air attributed to four of the major chakras, but there are other elements which I personally attribute to the remaining four chakras in animals.

Body systems

Chakras interact with the physical body through two major routes – the endocrine system and the nervous system. Each of the major chakras is associated with one of the seven endocrine glands that secrete chemical messengers or hormones to regulate the body. They are also linked to a group of nerves, called a plexus. The organs that lie in the vicinity of a chakra, or whose energy flows through it, link to that particular chakra.

It is worth mentioning here that chakras have a very complicated energy pattern. I have been privileged to experience this on several occasions. I have the honour of working from time to time alongside an animal osteopath and veterinary physiotherapists. On some of the more tricky cases I am invited to give healing whilst they are working with the soft tissue and the joints. On these occasions I am able to identify and describe the chakra patterns and the changes that they go through as these blockages rebalance and unwind. It is incredibly interesting work and we get some very good results together.

The chakras and their correspondences

The brachial major chakra or animal 'key' chakra

I have named this the brachial major chakra because anatomically it accesses the brachial plexus of nerves, an important network innervating the head, neck, chest and forelimbs. I have also added the title 'key', as many people find it an easier word to remember. I explain on page 99 why this chakra is a key to accessing the energy field of our pets when giving healing.

Through this chakra we can access all the other chakras. Often, when giving healing to suspicious or nervous pets, it is the nearest place

to the head that we can touch. This chakra also relates to a pet's relationship with the people in its life, so it is a very important area to channel healing through. The brachial major 'key' chakra lies at each side of the body at the top of the shoulder area. It is easier to find on bigger animals as the body area is larger, but even if you don't actually feel or sense it, particularly on small pets, just point a finger in the general area. The healing energy and your connection will be picked up by the chakra and the pet's energy field will do the rest!

The key chakra, or brachial major, is the main way to access the whole chakra system and the individual energy field for general rebalancing. In this illustration, the right hand is over this area. This chakra is also the animal/human spiritual gateway to the energy field and helps release emotional blockages. Through this chakra, we can also connect to the animal's healing energy being sent to us.

When treating smaller pets, try using your fingertips as the area is much smaller. Some pets don't like being touched so close to the head, in which case use one of the back chakras. Remember, you can make a healing connection by touching anywhere on the body, and if you can't touch, then you can make the connection by sending out your positive thoughts.

The left hand (placed on the head) is covering both the brow and the crown chakras – the fingers are over the brow chakra and the palm of the hand is over the crown chakra. These chakras connect the animal with the universal energy, and with our own thoughts and communications. This is a good area to give healing to for any head, neck, back or forelimb problem, and for general rebalancing.

You can see from this picture how much the dog Shona loves the healing; she has relaxed into a meditative state through the beneficial sensations that healing treatment brings. Animals can feel the same sensations during a healing treatment that humans can, and healing offers a deep inner peace.

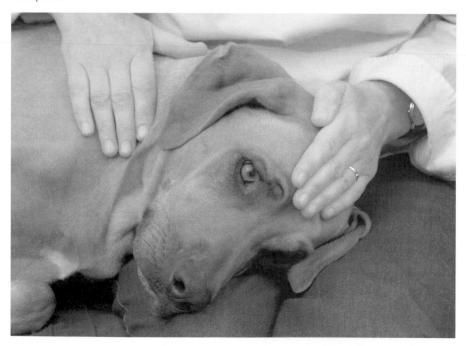

Location
This chakra lies at each side of the body in the shoulder area.

Chakra words for pet healing
Relationship with humans; natural instincts; awareness; transformation; darkness to light; revelation; healer; release.

Colour
Black.

Planet
Pluto.

Element
The universe.

Sense
The instincts.

Physical healing connection
Head, neck, chest, forelimbs (in four-legged animals).

Gemstone
Tiger's eye, snowflake obsidian, carnelian.

Affirmations
We are one you and I, both children of the universe. Let the healing energy hold us in its arms so that we both become stronger together.

The crown chakra

A pet's life force or soul energy reflects through the crown chakra into the aura and from here links with the universal intelligence. This chakra lies on top of the head between the ears. Although this is an important chakra over which to give healing, it is not always possible to do so directly with some pets. It means placing the hand over the head and some aggressive, poorly socialised or nervous pets may not be happy with this. Do not place the hand or fingers directly on to the head of a pet with head trauma. If your pet appears to worry or object to the head area being touched, ask your vet to check for any physical problems. Remember, you can also access this area through the brachial major or 'key' chakra in pets, and indeed from other chakras.

Location
The crown chakra is on top of the head between the ears.

Chakra words for pet healing
Soul; spirit; peace; linking to the universe; leadership.

Colour
Violet or purple, like a deep amethyst.

Planet
Uranus.

Element
Gold.

Sense
Thought, direction.

Physical healing connection
Brain, central nervous system, cranio-sacral system, spine, skin, fur or feathers.

Gemstone
Amethyst, diamond, white tourmaline, snowy quartz, celestite.

Affirmations
My wish for you is that you have peace and harmony. May you be at peace with the world and at one with the universe.

The brow chakra

If your pet allows you to touch the head, you can use this chakra to bless the pet and help it to feel the universal love (which I call God). It also links the pet with all of nature and when energies flow freely here it offers the animal the opportunity to understand the purpose and the meaning of everything in its life. The brow chakra is situated in the centre of the forehead above the eyes. Stressed, depressed and abused animals and birds will have a completely shut down brow chakra. If you look into the face of these traumatised souls, you will see the weakness and depletion of the brow chakra; the dull emptiness in their eyes is haunting and shaming to the human race.

Location
The brow chakra is across the forehead and above the eyes.

Chakra words for pet healing
Intuition; knowledge; understanding; insight; imagination; link to the universe; sense of belonging; teacher.

Colour
Indigo, a mixture of dark blue and violet.

Planet
Jupiter.

Element
Silver.

Sense
Intuition; extra-sensory perception; spirit-to-spirit communication.

Physical healing connection
Brain, face, endocrine system.

Gemstone
Amethyst, pearl, blue or white fluorite.

Affirmations
I promise you that I will always do my best for you. May you understand your life and be blessed in the knowledge that I care.

The throat chakra

Anyone who has had a pet or indeed had anything at all to do with animals and birds knows that they communicate with us and each other. Only humans use words. Some birds, such as parrots, can mimic words and sounds that they have heard, but only humans use them in a creative way to describe actions, thoughts and feelings. However, we should make no mistake that animals communicate in a very complex and comprehensive way. Sometimes their communication is soundless, which

Chakra positions on a dog. It is advisable to always give healing to a dog from behind so that you are not coming straight towards the head. I find that dogs prefer this approach. Depending on the dog, you may be able to lay your hands/fingers over all the chakra energy centres. If the dog appears unsure or uncomfortable about you being in a particular area, then leave that place and go somewhere else – healing is not a treatment to be forced on any creature.

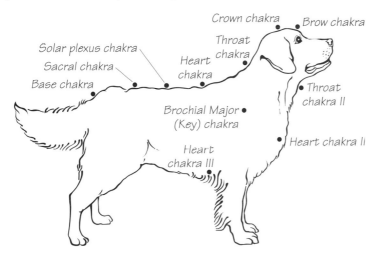

is why they need checking and handling every day to see if they are all right. Animals send out very strong communication signals and what we need to do, and where healing plays a huge role, is to listen. Healing also helps to release the pent-up energy of their frustrated, misunderstood or ignored communication.

The throat chakra is easily blocked when a pet struggles to convey information to the people in its life. It is an area which needs healing in animals who have been denied adequate contact with other animals or with people, as they then cannot express themselves naturally. For example, such animals might be from homes where they are abused or locked up alone for long periods, or from breeding places where the mother and offspring are kept in pens and cages without adequate human socialisation or caring. The throat chakra is found at the back of the neck or across the throat, but *never* hold, grip or pinch here. Hold your hand slightly below to give the healing. Some pets will not be happy for your hand to be here, so if they object then give that area a miss. Healing given to this chakra helps to prevent negative energy from affecting the body on a physical, mental and emotional level.

Location
The throat chakra is situated under the lower jaw across the throat, and at the back of the neck.

Chakra words for pet healing
Expression; communication; freedom; release; truth.

Colour
Blue, like a beautiful summer sky. Blue is the colour of the Aquarian age.

Planet
Mercury.

Element
The heavens.

Sense
Hearing; connection to the ether.

Physical healing connection
Ears, nose, mouth, teeth, thyroid gland, throat, shoulders, forelimbs.

Gemstone
Sapphire, turquoise, aquamarine, lapis lazuli.

Affirmations
Let me know how you feel. My aim is to hear your communication to me. My responsibility is to help you.

The heart chakra

The healer's own heart chakra is always fully open when giving healing, so this a very important area. We need to make sure that our own heart chakra is balanced before we give healing because it is the energy centre through which we give and receive love (see the chakra meditation on pages 92–3 as to how to do this). The heart chakra also plays an important role in the movement of spiritual energies from animal to human and vice versa. It is a good idea to give healing over this area as well as over the solar plexus chakra before and after any changes in the pet's life or routine.

The heart chakra is one to treat in both the mother and offspring after weaning, before you introduce newcomers into the house (give healing to all of them), after loss of a pet's companion, or after a change of home. It should definitely be given to a new pet in your life. Through this chakra, pets can let go of the sort of blockages that in a human would have resulted in tears. Animals do feel the same emotions that result in crying in humans, and when giving healing to an animal's heart chakra the people around often feel tearful as the sadness and frustration is released and hits them momentarily. Things including pain, shock, hospitalisation, loneliness, stress, boredom, mental and physical abuse and lack of love all shut down the energy flow through this chakra.

Location
The heart chakra is located in the back above the centre of the ribcage, the front of the chest and underneath the chest.

Chakra words for pet healing
Love; emotion; openness; forgiveness; sharing; relationships; balance.

Colour
Green – a bright emerald green.

Planet
Venus.

Element
Air.

Sense
Touch.

Physical healing connection
Heart, lungs, thymus, immune system.

Gemstone
Emerald, jade, tourmaline, azurite.

There are three heart chakra points on animals (see illustrations on pages 105, 110, 113 and 115): one on the top of the back, one in the front of the chest area below the neck and one under the chest, as shown in this photograph. If the pet is comfortable with this position, you can give healing through the heart chakra in this way. If not, try placing the hand over the top of the back as shown in the illustrations. You only need to treat one of the heart centres.

The heart chakra is an important place to give healing. When we are giving healing to another being, our own heart chakra is fully open to allow the healing energy connection. We open our heart chakra through the emotion of love, and this in turn links us to our pet on a very powerful healing wavelength and vibration.

The heart chakra on a pet will be depleted if it is unhappy, stressed, worried, sick or in pain, so give healing regularly here for these conditions in particular. The heart chakra is also the area on which to lay your hands to offer your love and let the pet know how much you care.

Heart chakra point on the back of a dog – for similar positions in cats, rabbits and birds see charts on pages 115, 110 and 113.

Affirmations

I love you with all my heart and soul. Feel my love; let it warm and protect you always. Take as much as you need, for my love has no limits and no boundaries.

The solar plexus chakra

Pets with digestive problems, those who are highly strung or worried, grieving pets and distressed animals, for example, will have energy blockage around the area of the solar plexus chakra. Disturbance in this chakra can also aggravate tummy upsets and behavioural problems. This chakra is affected by an animal's emotional state, so those who are stressed will have this chakra depleted. Often when healing in this area, there are tummy rumbling noises or release of wind as things begins to clear and there is an improved synergy of the vital organs. It is an important chakra to give healing to in working dogs after competitions as adrenalin in the system and the 'flight or fight' syndrome (which gives us humans a feeling of butterflies in the tummy) can block this chakra.

Location
The solar plexus chakra is in the centre of the back between the heart chakra and the sacral chakra.

Chakra words for pet healing
Survival; freedom of spirit; energy; sense of purpose; release of emotions; power; at ease.

Colour
Yellow – a golden yellow like the sun.

Planet
Mars.

Element
Fire.

Sense
Sight.

Physical healing connection
Whole body, stomach, kidneys, adrenal glands, liver, digestive system.

Gemstone
Amber, topaz, garnet, moonstone, rose quartz, alexandrite.

Affirmations
With my healing I aim to set your spirit free. I release your tears and suffering to the universe. I offer you calmness and strength.

The sacral chakra

This chakra links to the crown and brow chakras in terms of the healing balancing life force energy flowing through the spine. The sacral chakra is at the end of the cranio-sacral system and so it is affected by the rhythms of the body. Injuries and shock to the head and back will affect this chakra. I always find it malfunctioning in dogs with tight collars, head/face fitting collars and muzzles or in dogs who pull at the lead excessively. I have found that a great deal of chaotic emotional and mental energy can be released through giving healing through this chakra. It also has a role in security and nurturing. With any female animal that is in season, pregnant or having a false pregnancy, this is a useful area to treat, as it is also for any back problems.

Location
This chakra lies in the centre of the hip region of the spine.

Chakra words for pet healing
Security; sense of others; balance; internal equilibrium; pleasure.

Colour
Orange.

Planet
Moon.

Chakra positions on a rabbit. In my experience, rabbits will usually tolerate the hands positioned on either side of the shoulders, over the brachial major (key) chakra. Other areas I have used are the solar plexus, sacral and root chakras. Some will tolerate a gentle finger on the crown chakra. Rabbits can be given healing whilst in a cage or pen – see the illustration in Chapter 7 on page 121.

Chakra points are similar to those on other small animals, such as guinea pigs, gerbils, hamsters, rats, mice, chinchillas, etc.

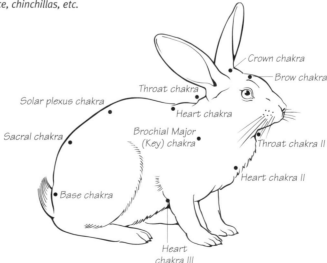

Element
Water.

Sense
Taste.

Physical healing connection
Reproductive system, lower back, adrenal glands, kidneys, lymphatic system.

Gemstone
Amber, citrine, topaz, jasper, ruby, moonstone.

Affirmations
We are joined together in the universal energy. I release your body from negative energy. Everything flows freely and peacefully through you.

Base chakra

This is the area where we give healing to 'ground' our pet, bringing it 'down to earth'. I find that most animals do not object to being touched here. The base or 'root' chakra is situated where the tail joins the body. Giving healing here also helps relieve the confusion we have created by restricting a pet's lifestyle regarding its responses to instinct and nature. Any physical problems, including those of the musculo-skeletal system, will affect this chakra. It will also be affected by any experience of separation or loss, and by weaning too early.

Location
The base chakra is at the end of the back where the tail starts.

Chakra words for pet healing
Stability; self-preservation; protection; grounding; strength; belonging.

Colour
Red.

Planet
Saturn.

Element
Earth.

Sense
Smell.

Physical healing connection
Legs (hind limbs in four-legged animals), whole skeleton, elimination system.

Gemstone

Bloodstone, ruby, agate, tiger's eye, garnet, onyx, alexandrite, smoky quartz.

Affirmations

Accept this healing. Feel as though you belong and have a purpose in life. May your life force be energised.

TOKI'S TUMOURS GET BETTER

Toki, a two-year-old Japanese chin, arrived in my clinic a very nervous and sick little dog. Helen, who brought her to me, was very worried because Toki had several tumours in a dangerous position on her thyroid gland and was due to have major surgery by a specialist throat vet. Helen had been warned that the tumours were very close to major blood supplies and there was a serious risk of haemorrhage during the operation. Toki was being treated with both conventional and homeopathic medication to prepare her for this tricky operation.

As well as the tumours, Toki had severe emotional problems because she was a rescue dog with a troubled past. She was totally lacking in confidence, always moving slowly with her tail hanging down and head drooping, holding her body in a cringing manner. While I made some notes, it was pitiful to watch Toki sitting in the corner of the room shaking. When I was ready to begin the healing, I laid my hand gently on to the back of her neck and she closed her eyes sighing deeply. Then she leant backwards on to my hand, still with her eyes tightly shut, as if in relief. We stayed like that for a quite a while and suddenly the little dog began to sway gently. I could feel tingling and heat build up under my hands over the heart chakra. Helen was sitting on a stool next to us and she told me that as the healing treatment progressed she began to get a buzzing sensation in her ears and a feeling of tightness in her head. When I took my hands off the dog, these sensations lessened then stopped. Afterwards Toki was very sleepy and Helen carried her out to the car.

A week later Helen reported a dramatic change in Toki's personality, describing it as if 'all the lights have gone on'. Toki had become much more confident and began asserting herself with the other dogs. Previously she had been far too nervous to go out into the garden but was now enjoying it, running round sniffing things and playing. In the kitchen she was even putting herself at the head of the queue at mealtimes, something that previously no one could ever imagine that she would have done. There was a spring in Toki's step and Helen was very pleased to find that she could reduce

112

the painkillers. The best news of all was that Helen thought the tumours were shrinking.

During the second healing visit, Toki was noticeably less nervous. After the third healing treatment, the tumours had shrunk so much that Helen had difficulty finding them. The personality change in Toki was now huge; she trotted in to greet me with her tail in the air and was really quite boisterous. In fact, in her newly developing relationship with the other dogs, Toki was now not afraid to answer back if something displeased her. Her coat had gone from dull to glossy and shiny and, yes, no other way to describe it, Toki was now cheerful.

The time came for Helen to visit the specialist vet who was due to perform the throat operation. At the end of a long and thorough examination, the vet turned to Helen and said, 'These tumours are now so tiny we can postpone the operation indefinitely.' The whole family were understandably over the moon and rushed out to buy a bottle of champagne to celebrate. Toki came for a couple more healing treatments, but then I too discharged her as she was so full of joie de vivre. Two years later I received a Christmas card from Helen to say that Toki continued to do well and even attempted a little growl when something didn't suit her! 'She is certainly a very different dog to when you first met her and we'll always be grateful for your help,' wrote Helen. I was so very grateful too that I had been able to offer spiritual and emotional help to that little dog.

Chakra positions on a bird. Birds will not usually like their heads or their tails being touched so I avoid these areas. I find that I can normally place my hand over the heart chakra on the back or the brachial major (key) chakra on the shoulders. Birds can be given healing whilst they are in a cage or pen – see the illustration in Chapter 7 on page 12.

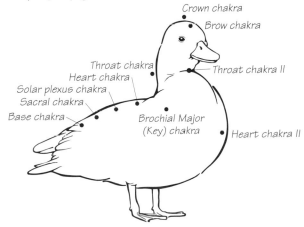

Crown chakra
Brow chakra
Throat chakra
Heart chakra
Solar plexus chakra
Sacral chakra
Base chakra
Throat chakra II
Brochial Major (Key) chakra
Heart chakra II

For various reasons there are times when you cannot touch or go near all the chakras. In these cases you will need to clear the whole chakra energy systems with your healing from just one point. This will work from any of the chakras.

- Have your hand or fingers on or near to the chakra you are able to connect with.
- Clear that chakra by focusing your mind on wanting to help your pet generally and send out your thoughts of love. The healing energy will automatically begin to flow.
- It may help you to visualise each chakra colour as you channel healing through them. A good suggestion is to have a series of cards with you, each one with the chakra colour on, so that you can look at it before you move on to that chakra.
- When you are ready to move on to the next chakra, *leave your hand where it is*, but in your *mind* concentrate on the next chakra that you wish to clear. Look at it to help you. You may feel a lot of heat or tingling as the body responds and you may even notice flickers in the new area or a few hairs or feathers standing up. These are all signs that the chakra is responding to the focus of your mind. Even if you do not notice anything, carry on because the healing will be received.
- Carry on in this way until you have focused with your mind on all the chakras.

My own chakra experience

For years I have been studying chakras and writing about them and although I could feel these energy centres over a body, the concept of the intertwining 'petals' revolving and opening up or closing down was something that I had to accept from descriptions in books or lectures. Then I had a very profound experience that left me in awe of those ancient teachers who knew so much, yet did not have our sophisticated technology. Perhaps that is why they had so much knowledge because they used the spiritual powers and potential that modern man has so neglected.

One of my cats was in the veterinary hospital and I had been told that he was probably terminally ill. He was on a drip in intensive care and I visited to give him healing. I could see that it brought him much comfort. Before I went to sleep, I sent him distant healing and prayed for him to have peace. I awoke in the early hours of the morning and found I was lying on my back. I was in that state between being fully awake yet not asleep, and in those few seconds I had my revelation.

The beauty and simplicity of hands-on healing is that it is creative and allows you to follow your intuition. In other words, listen with your healing energy to what the pet is asking of you. Wherever you feel the need to place your hand or hands is OK if the pet is happy with it because that is where you are being guided.

I was aware that my chest was open as though there was a big hole there. My mind panicked as the thought came into my head that perhaps I was ill, having a heart attack even. I put my hands up to touch my chest and felt a sensation like a wall in the air over it. It appeared to be about twelve inches away from my chest. Then I was aware that this wall had a shape like a huge funnel the width of my chest. As suddenly as the awareness came, I felt a movement – and in my mind I also saw what was happening. I saw and felt shapes like fingers entwining as they closed round each other and came down onto my chest. Then the realisation came without any doubt that I had experienced my heart chakra fully open to both send and receive love. With a flood of emotion, I knew that I had been linking to my beloved cat and that we had connected in our love for each other, both joined in healing. The experience left me feeling both amazed and humble, for there is a great deal that we do not fully understand. There is so much that our ancestors have pointed the way to; I believe healing is our journey to discovering the truth.

Chakra positions on a cat. There are two further heart chakra access points not illustrated here. One is in the centre of the chest and the other underneath the body. For a position guide, see the photo on page 108 and the dog chakra chart on page 105.

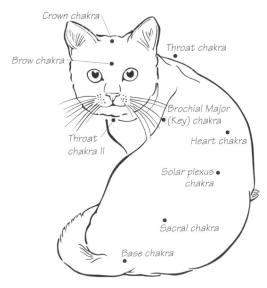

Crown chakra

Throat chakra

Brow chakra

Brochial Major (Key) chakra

Throat chakra II

Heart chakra

Solar plexus chakra

Sacral chakra

Base chakra

7 The healing experience for you and your pet

If you could shift your viewpoint for just a moment, as you grow still and silent within, without a thought or care, without a worry or desire, you might begin to feel a power tingling in your fingertips. . . .

Silvia Hartmann-Kent

When I am giving healing I frequently get asked, 'Can anyone do this?' All people on this earth can be healers and I have written this book to offer help and guidance to pet owners so that they can understand how to go about giving healing and realise their potential. Everyone has the free will to either heal or hurt; it is as simple as that. It is the most natural thing in the world for animal lovers to want to help a troubled creature. This basic instinct can be developed by healers so that they are able to be strong channels when linking with the universal mind. Deep healing can then be offered to any animal in need. Clients also often say to me, 'But how do I know if I'm doing any good?' With the right focus and the intent to heal it *always* makes a difference on some level.

One such person, an elderly lady, was overcome when she touched her very sick dog to try to give it some healing. She described 'a sunny feeling' in her body and hand and a 'surge of lightness through the dog's back'. It meant such a lot to her to be able to carry on helping him after I had left.

Anyone can channel healing, for we are all from the same source of universal energy and we are all connected to the whole. We were born with permission to tap into the source of healing and when we choose to do so we can make a difference on many levels. Until you try you will not know how gifted you are as a healer or how much natural ability you have – you may be very pleasantly surprised. Everyone differs in their ability to feel and work with the energy blueprint and to harness its potential; therefore not everyone will be able to work as deeply and as powerfully as is possible. Some find it easier than others to adjust to the subtle energy information during a healing session. From my own experience many people go on to take courses in healing once they have

had a go and realised that they have had an effect, and want to find out more.

The guidelines in this book are intended for use only with your own animals. To practise as a professional healer and become a member of a recognised association with the relevant accreditation involves training for at least a couple of years. It is a good idea to have healing yourself so that you can experience what it feels like – animals will have the same sensations and feelings. My advice is to always use a registered healer as a guideline to their professional status and integrity. *And remember that healing should never be used as a substitute for veterinary care.* If you are concerned in any way about the pet's health or well-being, always seek advice from a vet; otherwise a minor issue could become a major one.

A healing life

Incorporating natural healthcare and organic food into our healing lives is a good idea because this avoids the chemicals, toxins and side-effects that many other products or medications have. The more in balance our bodies are, the more effective our healing can be. Factory-farmed food should be avoided for our energy fields to be bright and healthy. These words by Alice Walker ring very true for me: 'We are not spiritually unconnected from the drugs we take or from the pain and suffering that goes in their making.'

The healing experience

The earth's powerful forces of weather, energy fields, seasons and other natural phenomena are not such a mystery to animals as they are for us humans. In the same way these creatures intuitively recognise healing – they know what it is and how it can help them because they naturally understand the source and the power that is available to us all, whatever species we belong to.

Many of my clients tell me that once they start giving healing it changes their lives and this can be difficult for them to describe. People say that they understand the animal better, feel closer to it and more bonded. Fiona is typical of many people who have written to me: 'I never thought that I would be able to help Oscar my elderly cat. The healing has changed my view on life and brought us so much closer together.' If we are serious about being healers, our outlook changes as the healing takes us onto a new pathway in life.

> Giving healing is a living prayer – it is the language of the soul.

Healing is not something to do just once, but needs to become a regular part of our lives, and to be in the forefront of our thinking, our reasoning and our understanding of this world of ours. When we open ourselves up to healing, many changes take place in our energy field and our aura as we become more sensitive and more receptive. That is why once people start to practise healing they frequently feel the need to make changes in other areas of their lives, re-evaluate relationships and friendships, places they visit, and their priorities. *Being a healer is a lifestyle, not just a concept.*

It takes practice, patience and time to develop efficient healing skills and gain confidence in energy communication. The more healing we give, the stronger it becomes. Regular meditation is very important to help train the mind to work on a more sensitive level and not to wander, and to begin to sense energy messages. Over a period of time, as the healing potential develops different levels of awareness and understanding will unfold for you. Giving healing to your pet is to experience, and be guided along, a very special journey.

Healing time

When you give healing it is important not to be in a hurry and to make sure that the environment is as calm as possible, otherwise you will be distracted and the healing connection will not be very effective. The pet will pick up on your agitation too and put up barriers to your own chaotic emotions, which will block any healing energy from being received. Use the following points as a guideline for your healing time.

- Choose a time when you are not in a hurry and are unlikely to be disturbed. Thirty minutes is a reasonable time to set aside. Make sure you feel at ease. You may wish to play some soothing music to help create an atmosphere of calm.

- The pet should ideally be as relaxed as possible and resting, not in activity or play mode. Healing should not take place around a time when normally something happens in the animal's daily routine – for example, someone coming home, the pet going out or its feeding time.

- Televisions, telephones, etc, should be switched off so that you are not disturbed.

- Remove magnetic collars and rugs from pets, also any magnetic wrist bands you might be wearing. This is so that nothing disturbs the energy connection between you both.

- It is very important that you are both comfortable. It may be possible to have the pet on your lap or next to you on a sofa or chair. Other pets will need to be given healing as they lie on a bed on the ground or in a pen or cage (see page 121).

- With animals that need regulated environments, such as reptiles, don't disturb this but see how you can fit the healing in with its essential needs.

Times when healing should not be given

There are times when healing should not be given because not only will the energy connection be poor but the pet will sense the human disturbed energy and be unreceptive. These times include the following:

- After any alcoholic drink – the mind will not be clear for focusing on the healing. Animals can also be disturbed by the energies we give off in this situation.

- When taking mind-influencing medication or drugs for the same reason as above.

- During times of extreme stress – the healer needs to be calm and relaxed for the healing channels to be fully open.

- When health is poor, because the healer's energy field will be weak and therefore will not make a strong healing energy connection.

- During periods of fatigue for the same reason as above.

- When depressed, as depression creates negative energy and is therefore counterproductive to offering healing to others.

Hand positions for healing

1. You can use one or two hands, depending on the size of the pet and the area you are working over (either a chakra, as detailed in Chapter 6, or areas picked up from a body scan, as described on pages 125–6). For smaller pets, healing can be given by making contact with a fingertip or tips. The touch must always be very gentle – like a

Your healing touch
The contact from your hand to make the healing connection should be very gentle and light – as soft as a butterfly landing on the pet's body. Never press down or allow the hand to rest on the body as it can be uncomfortable for the pet. Avoid areas where the pet is not happy for you to touch.

butterfly landing. If you have long fingernails, check they are not irritating or digging into the animal's body.

2. Sometimes it may not be possible to touch the pet to give healing. In this case the hand can be held above the body. All around the animal, as with humans, is an invisible force field that consists of subtle energies – the aura. Healers can work on these fields by holding the hand away from the body. Healing can even be successfully given from some distance away by pointing a hand or both hands towards the animal in need. For pets that can't be touched, whether due to illness, temperament or environmental requirements, give the healing from a distance that is safe for both of you. Sending out love creates a powerful healing energy connection.

3. Small animals or the very young can be given healing by cupping them in the hands. As soon as you start to focus on sending healing, the energy will flow from your fingertips and through the palm of the hand into the body you are holding.

4. Healing can be given to fish by either touching the surface of the

Water transports energy, so by touching the surface of the water with clean hands, beneficial healing energy can be transmitted to fish.

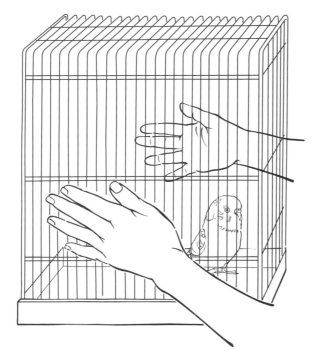

Place the hands around a cage, pen or box to give healing to pets that are not happy with being handled, or who are fidgety because they are sick or injured. Healing energy travels from the hands to the pet's body, reaching any area in need and at whatever level is necessary (mental, emotional or physical).

water with a finger or, if the fish is lying near to the surface, holding a finger in the water next to the fish (without touching it). Energy travels through water and the healing benefits will reach the fish in this way.

5. Animals and birds that are unhappy with being handled can be left in a cage and the hands placed around it to direct healing to them.

Beginning the healing treatment and tuning in

When we give healing we are embarking on a wonderful journey of discovery and spiritual adventure.

Our mental and emotional circumstances are very important when we begin giving healing and animals are very sensitive to what we are thinking and how we are feeling. The two 'keys', which will activate the healing and create the link to the source, come from our positive intentions and sending out love to the animal with a real passion in our hearts, so much so that we may feel overwhelmed. We can never offer too much love when we give healing to another creature. It is really

121

important to push all other thoughts away from the mind other than ones of love and a desire to help. Although healing can produce some dramatic results, remember it is not a cure-all; you are offering help on whatever level is possible and we have no control over this. Healing is, however, always received on some level and the outcome will depend both on the age of the pet and the nature of the problem.

Healing can be targeted to specific areas, such as a wound, problem joint or where there has been surgery. Science has shown that hands-on healing helps speed up the repair of cells. Because healing releases endorphins in the body (which have an effect like morphine) it plays an important role in natural pain relief, helping alongside pain medication and remedies.

   Be careful not to actually touch open wounds, sore places or sites of recent surgery to give the healing, instead keeping the hands above the body.

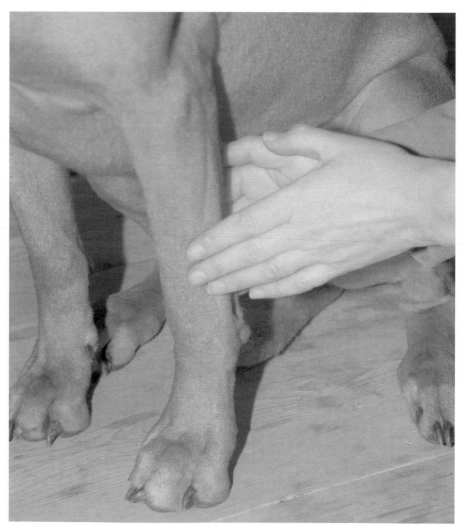

Treatment tips and a summary of how to give healing ✓

Healing can be given via the hands through the chakras, over individual areas such as a wound or a joint, or over areas of energy blockage sensed when making a body scan with the hands. Healing can also be given by holding the hands above the body, or sent from a distance, even from many miles away.

Starting the treatment

Remember we are born already attuned to the universal source of healing. All that is required of us is to lay a hand on our pet and say, 'I accept and I'm here to work with the healing power.'

The healing keys

Focusing the mind to send out positive thoughts, and sending out all the love from your heart – really wanting to help – are the two keys to making a strong healing connection. Thoughts influence healing energy – positive thoughts of love, harmony and peace create a strong energy connection. Keep concentrating on being the link between the pet and the universal source of healing energy.

Permission to heal

Ask the pet's permission to let the healing through – signs of acceptance include a sense of your hand blending with the pet's body, and a peaceful atmosphere around you both. After the healing treatment, thank the healing source for working with you and your pet. It doesn't matter what your personal beliefs are about where the healing comes from.

Our thoughts

Thoughts have a powerful vitality of their own. A strong desire to help and make changes creates a huge shift in the operation and function of the electromagnetic field of the body. Thinking negative thoughts makes the energy field go weak and also closes the mind. These negative thoughts are picked up by our pets and can become like a black cloud around them. Negative thoughts affect our own health and people who smile a lot and look on the bright side of things are known to suffer less from ailments than people who are pessimistic, such is the power of thought. Thinking positive thoughts creates a surge in beneficial energy and to be an effective healer the mind needs to be open and accepting.

It sounds a bit complicated but is easy really – just relax with your pet, concentrate on sending out loving thoughts and it will all come

together. The healing will begin to flow. Healing energy follows thought, so send out wishes that your pet can be helped on whatever level is possible. Allow your thoughts to blend with the pet on a general level, rather than concentrating on one place because the place where you think the cause of problem is may not be correct. Of course, if you are targeting a wound, for example, then you can send out positive thoughts to that individual area as well as treating the body generally. With an open mind, ask for the healing to go wherever it is needed and wait for some signs that the healing is coming through and being registered by the pet (see list on pages 126–8). Even if you do not notice anything in particular, don't give up because healing always has some effect, providing you keep the love pouring out and your mind is sending thoughts of wanting to help.

As with everything in life, practice makes perfect and it does take time to build up the lines of healing communication.

The benefits of healing for our pets

- Healing energy is available for everyone to tap into. The energy field of all living beings is a continually changing network of information. What happens on one level in the animal always affects the whole. When we give healing we work holistically to help physically, mentally, emotionally and, of course, spiritually.

- Healing is safe for all conditions and problems and doesn't have any harmful side-effects.

- Healing flows throughout the whole physical body as well as the mental and emotional state.

- Healing has been proved to help preventatively.

- Healing can result in an improved sense of well-being and give a feeling of peacefulness.

- Healing helps other treatments and therapies to work more deeply.

- Healing may be able to help when everything else has failed.

- Healing is sometimes successful with just one treatment, although more often a few treatments are necessary depending on the problem.

Healing and the endorphin effect

It is well documented that endorphins, biochemicals naturally produced by the body, are released during healing. Chemically similar to opium and morphine, they are the reason why healing can help so much with pain relief. We know that in extreme conditions the body is capable of producing endorphins far stronger than chemical morphine. It is worth noting that stressed animals can take part in behaviour to release endorphins to numb mental and emotional pain as well as physical pain. An example of this is excessive grooming or hyperactive/repetitive behaviour. This is another reason why any pet behaving out of character or abnormally should be seen by a vet.

Endorphins are known to work towards the repair of wounded and diseased tissue and may also boost the immune system. They create physical feelings of well-being, which become sensations of emotional, mental and psychological health and happiness. Very importantly, endorphins are known to create euphoria and a sense of spiritual connection with the universe. We can now see just how far-reaching the benefits of healing are for our pets because of the powerful effects endorphins have when activated by a healing treatment. The response and frequent improvements to an animal's health and behaviour after healing speak for themselves. The terminally ill pet will also benefit tremendously from the calming sensations of the endorphins released by the healing. And the wonderful thing is that all these benefits are something that you can offer your own animal. Sometimes the effect of healing is calming and sometimes stimulating, depending on the response of the body and its needs. Often both of these responses can be observed in one treatment.

'The healer is the link between the universal source of energy and the energy field of the pet'

Intuitive healing

The whole body scan

Some people are naturally intuitive with healing, which means that they can 'sense' or 'feel' problem areas or blockages over a pet's body. With time you should begin to become more confident about what you are feeling and the healing results you are getting. The hands can be used to scan over the body – hold them slightly above and move slowly around the pet – and energetic information can be received in this way. You may

find yourself almost drifting off or even becoming sleepy. This is because when we work with healing energy a much deeper involvement within our brain takes place than normal. With different animals, the energy can give a variety of sensations – the reaction will be stronger in some than in others because every being has a natural energy rhythm that pulls energy to it. It is this 'pull' that we can feel as a strong sensation in many cases; at other times there is a less dramatic response because the 'pull' is less defined.

As you scan and detect areas of energy blockage, you may pick up corresponding sensations under your hands, such as unusual heat, cold, tingling or pulsing, or your hand may feel 'drawn in' to an area or pushed away. When you find such spots, keep the hand over these places until the areas change and feel more normal again. In this way you are using your hands as a magnet to release congestion in the electromagnetic field of the animal and to rebalance the flow of energy. Each time you give healing check the areas where you found energy blockage. If the blockage keeps recurring, think about what the cause could be. Remember that with healing we can pick up health problems from the aura before symptoms appear. Perhaps lifestyle changes need to be addressed or perhaps there is some stress involved. Perhaps a more natural diet would help or perhaps there is discomfort somewhere in the body which needs investigation.

Young animals

Young animals can be very fidgety and lack concentration. However, they also tire quickly and sleep deeply so that gives a good window of opportunity for some healing. It is a very good idea to give healing to the young to help boost the immune system and for the feel-good factor. Healing can be safely given to even the newly born if there is a problem, either by gentle fingertip touch or if appropriate by holding it in the hands.

What animals can feel during healing

Animals can physically feel what we do – perhaps even more as their senses are more acute than ours. Initially they can feel heat or tingling from the healer's hands as the healing connection stimulates and intensifies the electromagnetic field. On very rare occasions an animal

The healing
experience for you
and your pet

may be momentarily wary of these sensations but in my experience they soon settle down to enjoy it. Healing is a beneficial and safe therapy and a rewarding experience, no matter what the problem is because it flows on a vibration of purest love.

Three sets of information give us a clue as to the many things animals can feel during healing.

- Often other people present in the room during healing will talk about things that they are suddenly feeling or sensing. I regard this as a reflection of what is happening within the pet.

- The pet's reaction – it is obvious by watching facial expressions and body language that a response to something unusual is taking place.

- Feedback from humans who have had healing – animals can be expected to feel the same things as a human would during healing because they consist of blood, flesh, bone and nerve endings in just the same way as we do.

These are some of the things the pet may feel during healing:

- Tingling or buzzing feeling in a part of the body or generally all over.

- Light-headedness, a 'floaty' feeling or the mind wandering.

- Sleepiness or extreme tiredness, drowsiness.

- Shivering.

- Heat in parts of the body or all over.

- Flickering or twinges in the limbs (kinetic releases of energy).

- Quicker or slower breathing rate.

- Emotional upset or tearfulness. Animals cannot cry like humans, of course, but they can feel upset and sad just like we do and this creates disturbed energy. Healing allows it the chance to discharge and flow better.

- Heaviness in one or more limbs.

- Pleasant warmth and cosiness.

- Total relaxation.

Keep a close watch over the pet during healing. If they become shivery – although this is rare – stop and make sure that they are warm enough. However, shivering is also a sign of fever or pain so consider whether any problem your pet has is illness-related. Has the pet been checked by a vet recently? If not, it would be advisable to seek advice. Hot spots will cool down as the healing rebalances the body and disturbed energy is

DAFFODIL THE DUCK

Daffodil had been to our clinic at Holistic Pets a couple of times before. People were always surprised to see her in the physiotherapy room because Daffodil is a white duck! We explained that ducks are no different to other animals in the fact that they have muscles and bones, so physiotherapy can be of real benefit. Daffodil had a limp and physiotherapy was helping with that problem. The woman who brought her in requested that Daffodil had some healing as well because she was on medication for a beak infection which had turned it green. She was altogether in quite a sorry state.

I asked for Daffodil to be left in her carrying cage as she tended to wriggle about a lot and I thought that she would be more settled in there, and I sat next to it on the treatment couch. The cage was a fairly large wire one of the type used for transporting cats and Daffodil stood in the middle of it looking around, cocking her head from side to side. I settled myself into a comfortable position and, placing my hands around the cage, tuned in to give the healing. I could see by the look in her eye that she was registering the energy sensations and then suddenly she fluffed her feathers right up – and then dropped to the floor of the cage, just lying there on her side with her eyes tightly shut. I must say that momentarily I was a bit alarmed but very quickly I realised what had happened. I had spent the morning giving healing to three big horses and my energy field was really powered up. I had forgotten to take a break before giving healing to the duck – a much smaller energy field – and she had been a bit overwhelmed by it. Hence she was now fast asleep on the floor of her cage! I carried on with the healing for about another ten minutes for I knew that she was perfectly safe.

After I had finished she slowly opened an eye and blinked cheekily at me as if to say, 'Had you worried there for a minute didn't I?' then shut it quickly again! The woman who brought her in was highly amused. She called us a week later to report that Daffodil had slept all the way home, but the next morning she was very cheerful and chatty. When people ask if healing works and if it is a powerful therapy for all types of creatures, my colleagues always laugh and tell the story of Daffodil!

The healing
experience for you
and your pet

released. Other sensations will cease when the healing session ends, with the exception of peacefulness, calm and pain relief. How long can these particular states be expected to continue? Depending on the condition, they could last for several hours or up to a few days and often there may be more permanent benefits.

What the healer can feel

Sometimes initially people get very strong physical sensations as they pick up not only reflected energy from the animal but their own responses to working with this type of energy. However, I tell them they don't want to be feeling too much too strongly because then it becomes distracting. The healer needs to be in control of their response and the way to do this is to aim to get the sensations in the mind and not the body. How do you do this? Quite simply, tell your mind that is how you wish to work and it will happen! Remember my comments earlier in the book that thought creates a strong pattern of energy, so what you think becomes part of the healing process. If initially you become light-headed or emotional, then stop, take a break and start again.

Healers may feel heat or tingling in their hands and that is perfectly all right to work with. Any other sensations should be guarded against; after all, the aim is healing for our pets, not to make ourselves the centre of interest. Do not worry if you do not feel anything at all when giving healing – some people don't have these sensations but the healing will be effective nevertheless. Your love is what counts. As you develop and become more in tune and intuitive, then you should become aware of more subtle energy movements and patterns. You may feel the following:

- Heat in the palms of the hands or fingers.

- A sensation of the hand being drawn into the pet's body. This is the response from the magnetic field.

- A feeling of the hand becoming 'light' as your energy blends with the pet.

- Tingling, pulsing or feelings like little electric shocks in the fingers – either in all of them or just one or two. These sensations will usually come and go as the healing energy scans through the body. When it is rebalanced the sensations usually cease.

- Awareness of hot or cold spots on the animal's body.

A healing tip

If the pet becomes fidgety and gets up or walks away, leave it for another time. We *always* offer healing, asking for permission to continue, and should never force it onto another being. Healing is received very quickly too, so that short space of time may have been enough.

Responses and reactions

Because healing is non-invasive and gentle, the responses and reactions are not unpleasant and can be difficult to detect because they are subtle. The more healing we practise, the easier it becomes to interpret the signs.

Animals will often position themselves to work more efficiently with the healer's hands. They will move themselves around so that certain parts of their body are under your hands – areas that they feel need the healing directed to. Often they will push their bodies into the hands during healing and the healer often feels as though they are being drawn towards them. If this happens, take your cue from them and direct the healing where they guide you to before moving on to other areas if required. This is their magnetic field interacting with yours.

Some animals just 'plug in' to the healing and reach the alpha state very quickly, obviously enjoying the energy sensations within their bodies and minds. Sometimes the animal will look at a certain area on the body or point to it with their nose – again go where they ask you to. The healing treatment is for their benefit and they know what is best for them. If there are wounds, sore or tender places or sites of recent surgery, keep the hands above those places and do not touch them directly.

Here are some of the responses and reactions that I have experienced over the years when giving healing to animals.

All pets

- Peaceful effect – the pet shows signs of sleepiness, head drooping, eyes flickering closed, body very relaxed

Dogs/cats/small furries/any four-legged pet

- Face and muzzle looks relaxed
- Quivering nostrils and whiskers

- Muscle twitches (kinetic releases of energy), skin rippling
- Initially may want to lick the feet if they feel tingly
- Stretching out
- Intermittent tail wagging/tail movements due to pleasant sensations
- Sighing
- Licking lips
- Tongue sticking out
- A sneeze or two (clearing the sinus)
- Changes in skin temperature. Can vary in different parts of the body
- Momentary quivering
- Increased or decreased respiratory (breathing) rate
- Looking round at body or healer's hands
- Yawning
- Vocal noises, purring, gentle grunts
- Body looks very relaxed
- Changes in the fur. The skin is the body's largest organ and fur grows from it so as the skin responds to the healing visible signs are in fur changes. The fur may stand up in places or be flatter to the body than before healing and the tail may even fluff up. There may be slight dampness in places and often there is an added lustre to the coat after healing.
- When healing has a stimulating effect the pet may be thirsty or hungry

Birds

- Making vocal noises
- Opening beak
- Very relaxed and leaning against the hand
- Stretching wings, or holding wings out to the sides
- Resting head on one side
- Fluffing feathers out
- Looking intently into the healer's eyes
- Colour changes to skin in areas where not much feather coverage
- Becoming thirsty or hungry

Fish

- Swimming pattern changes – usually initially slows down
- Darting up and down as healing produces stimulating effects
- Gulping a few times as healing flows through the water
- Becoming hungry

Reptiles

- Tongue flicking
- Rippling in the skin
- Stretching limbs
- Tail movements
- Increased activity afterwards due to stimulation
- Becoming hungry or thirsty

Note: Reptiles are not considered suitable as pets due to their special environmental, social and dietary needs. I include healing with reptiles in this book as information for conservationists involved in their care.

Signs of pain

It is worth mentioning here how to recognise some signs of pain in pets so that a vet can be consulted as early as possible. These include changes in behaviour, going off food, unwillingness to be touched, groaning noises, frequent looking round at the body for no reason, excessive limb-licking and chewing, teeth-grinding, hiding, crying on moving, reluctance to exercise, head pressing or rubbing, excessive panting and depression. Healing works well alongside conventional medicine for pain relief but should never be used instead of it.

THE HOTEL CAT

I remember once noticing a cat lying on a chair in a hotel foyer. I picked up intuitively that she suffered from frequent headaches and sat down next to her to offer healing. The receptionist told me that the cat was temperamental with visitors and so there was a question mark over her future. When I explained that she suffered from bouts of head pain, they saw her attitude in a different light and set about trying to help her. A veterinary examination subsequently revealed an ulcer in the eye, which would have to be removed by surgery. The ulcer had indeed caused the cat a lot of pain and naturally made her feel grumpy about having her head touched.

Things that healing can't do

If the pet's problem is related to or caused by stress, boredom or neglect, or if its natural needs are not being met, then healing benefits will not be lasting. Healing, for example, won't make up for lack of exercise, stimulation or company. There may be some changes that you need to make to the pet's lifestyle or diet. Some additives and colourings in pet foods can cause health and personality problems, and chemicals in the home and garden can make pets ill or behave oddly. An honest assessment needs to be made by the animal care-giver about improvements that would help both in physical terms and with behaviour, as well as offering regular healing.

I'm often called to give healing when everything else has failed and people expect a miracle! Healing can, and often does, produce sudden and dramatic changes, but more often than not improvements are gradual, especially with chronic conditions, and show over a period of time. In my experience acute conditions, especially in the younger pet, can respond most quickly. Healing is not going to be able to restore vitality to badly damaged tissue or restore full function to diseased body parts. Surgery is often the only option. Healing helps, however, to stimulate the body to recovery and repair where possible, which in many cases results in better health.

Remember the body and its emotional/mental/spiritual combination is very complex and healing *always* works on some level, even if it is not what we hoped for. Perhaps the spiritual level is the one reached but as this will benefit the life force, or soul energy, for eternity, then we should always consider the bigger picture. Physical healing is not always part of the possible current situation.

Healing cannot reverse severe organ or tissue damage or degeneration – there is a time span for the physical life to end for all living things.

Healing won't change a dog into a cat

Healing won't change the pet into something that it is not by changing a fundamental personality. For example, healing won't make an aggressive dog into a laid back pussy-cat, or turn a nervous cat suddenly into an extrovert. Healing aims to help the animal get in touch with who it is and to express itself better, bringing out the more positive aspects of the character and producing a sense of contentment. Often regular healing does result in the pet behaving in a more acceptable way for us. As

explained in Chapter 3, the early upbringing of dogs and cats plays a vital role in their later adult behaviour and relationships, not just with humans but each other. Genetic disposition and the type of breed also determine some character traits. Healing aims to help our pets realise their best potential.

Distant or 'remote' healing

Healing energy is not limited by distance, time or space. It is everywhere.

Healing can be given very effectively from a distance, remotely from the person or animal that we wish to help, and this is something that healers do frequently. Healing energies originate from a source outside of the physical body and this energy is available to everyone, wherever they are, even if they are not with the person or animal they wish to give the healing to. The healer's influence in reaching a receiver through a dimension other than the physical has been well documented in studies with humans, plants and animals. This works because there is no point at which the energy fields emitted from living beings actually cease. The energy gets weaker as it gets further from the body, but we are still able to pick up an individual energy signature to make the healing connection. In this way healing can be sent to pets who are not with us for some reason – perhaps they are in a boarding place or in hospital, living with a friend or relative or have even been re-homed. We can also send healing to the millions of animals in this world who are living in fear and distress. When we concentrate on one particular pet, the healing reaches that pet's individual energy field; when we concentrate on animals in general, the healing source links with all of those in need.

Sending out healing

To send out healing from a distance, you need to sit quietly and fill the mind with loving thoughts for the animal you wish to reach and envision it there with you. Make up your own healing prayer – some words of love that you wish to say and include the pet's name. When these words are clear in your mind, ask the source of healing to carry them to the animal – it doesn't matter where or what you think that source is. Your love and strong thoughts create the healing bond and this energy can be very powerful in its benefits. People who are sent distant or remote

healing can testify as to how good it feels and there is no reason to think that it is otherwise with our pets.

If you wish to send healing to animals in general, then envision light flowing out from every part of your body. Fill your mind with thoughts that you wish to reach every animal in need, no matter where it is. We have no control over how the healing will be received or the way it can work, but it does reach these suffering souls. The world's animals need every one of us to be in the habit of finding a few moments each day to send out healing thoughts. Just a minute or two spent can be put to good use, wherever we are, sending out love and compassion and thereby creating a wave of light energy. This is an easy but powerful way to reach all the planet's creatures – isn't it the very least we can do?

DUKE, A VERY SPECIAL KITTEN

There was the usual pile of letters on the mat that Saturday morning, but one stood out. The postmark on the small envelope gave me a clue that it related to a very sick kitten. I took the letter up to my healing room and opened it. Inside was a photo with a yellow piece of paper and on it was written 'Duke's fur'. I unfolded the paper and felt very emotional as I saw the piece of black fur. It seemed very poignant somehow, such a very tiny piece of fur from such a tiny kitten struggling to stay alive, just 14 weeks old.

Duke was the only black kitten in a litter of eight Orientals; the others were all a mixture of tabby, spotted and tortie points. His dramatic colour made him stand out, especially as he was the biggest and strongest of the kittens. Although we had never met, Kathy, the woman who had bred Duke, and I struck up a friendship over the telephone, based on our love of cats. One day she wrote to me, sending a photo of Duke and asking me to pray for him as he had collapsed a couple of days after he had arrived in his new home. He was very sick. I arranged for a snippet of fur to be sent so that I could pick up his energy field better to do distant healing and it was that which had arrived in the post. When I had looked at Duke's photo I had felt a tremendous foreboding. I could see in that tiny pointed face that inside him was a wise old soul. He also looked sad, I thought, as if he knew that he wasn't going to make it, and having enjoyed the friendship, fun and love of his human and cat family, he didn't want to leave just yet. The energy field I picked up from the fur was weak and after a while I experienced a sudden and huge movement of energy, which moved in a circular fashion through my

fingers before stopping. I went back some time later to hold the fur again but I knew that Duke had just passed away – what I was feeling was still *him,* his energy signature, but on another plane. I put the fur down on my healing table. It looked so small, so soft and such a pretty shiny shade of black, and I prayed then for all kittens who died.

Later Kathy rang me to confirm that Duke had indeed died. The vet had suspected the viral disease FIP (feline infectious peritasitis) from blood tests, possibly brought on by the stress of the journey to the new home. FIP is tragically a terminal illness and Duke had been booked to be put to sleep on that Saturday at 12.20pm, just a week after he had arrived. Naturally his new family were absolutely devastated. Just before they were due to leave the house to take Duke to the vet, he deteriorated so much that they called the vet to come to the house instead. Before the vet arrived, Duke crawled out of his bed and lay on the floor – then he just passed away. It was exactly 12.20pm, around the time that I had been sending out my distant healing. I feel that Duke took the spiritual strength and peace it gave him to go on to his final journey and leave his young body.

I spoke to Kathy for a long time about the trauma of losing Duke and she said that she felt guilty that she had sent Duke away to die. His death had come as a terrible shock, especially as he had been the biggest and strongest kitten in the litter. Kathy confessed that when the couple had come to collect Duke and take him to his new home, she'd had the overwhelming urge to stop them. She felt uneasy about him going, even though the couple were experienced with cats and offered the very best of homes. Duke had been inoculated and pronounced fully fit by a vet and so at the time Kathy didn't have a valid reason for stopping the kitten going away, but she now realised that she'd had a sixth sense that tragedy was about to happen.

I never met Duke, yet I felt his presence from his tiny piece of fur, met his gaze from that photo and loved him. Yes, he was very special and many months on I still touch his fur and pray for him that his life now is easy and that he is happy playing with the many thousands of kittens who never grew up to be cats.

Be unselfish with healing

With breeding, competition or show animals, healing may well result in more success due to an improved sense of well-being. The love in our hearts is what activates healing energy, but if we give healing expecting a material benefit for ourselves that is not an honest basis for true communication with our pets. The 'achievement' of winning rosettes and cups is a human aspiration and bears no relation to the spiritual life of the animal (or ours for that matter), neither has it a place in the healing ambition of wanting to help on a profound and meaningful level. The human ego needs to take a back seat for healing to be truly supportive.

137

8 Using crystals and gemstones as a healing aid

Nothing should ever be treated with contempt. Whatever it is that lives, a man, a tree, or a bird, should be touched gently because time is short. Civilisation is another word for respect for life . . . .

Elisabeth Goudge

Most people have some natural stones in their possession, perhaps a favourite item of jewellery or a piece of crystal to catch the light and reflect rainbow colours around the room. The colour of the crystal is linked to its atomic structure and plays a role in the frequency with which it vibrates. The colour that our eyes see in a crystal is the colour of the light it reflects. For example, an amethyst absorbs every colour except purple, an aquamarine absorbs every colour except blue, and so on.

We are often drawn to gemstones and crystal with qualities that are beneficial for us at that particular time. We can make use of their natural energy with our pet healing. It may be that you already have in your possession a stone that is suitable as a healing aid. When we look at a stone, we may think that it is a solid inanimate object, but they actually possess resonant properties, which means that within them are minute movements of energy. Each crystal or gemstone has an individual energy property to help with different conditions.

How crystal healing works with our pets

Biologists now know that in many cells of the body, both human and animal, there are living liquid crystals with subtle vibrations similar to those found in crystal stones. When we use crystal stones in healing, their vibrations link with the energy within the tissues of our pets. So by using them we can enhance the therapeutic effects. Sometimes the crystals introduce a new vibration into the body to help fine-tune the energies

further. Crystals link with our healing energy to send out a vibration, which amplifies the power of the healer's intent (mind energy).

It is said that the people of the great legendary continent of Atlantis, dating from at least 150,000BC, developed the art of healing with gems and crystals. Certainly many civilisations have used crystal power for their benefit in many different ways and liquid crystals are used today in technology ranging from timepieces, transportation, medical equipment, electricity and computer equipment.

It's really important in all forms of healing, including healing with gemstones, that the healer's intent is to help for totally unselfish reasons. When we use gemstones we need to tune into the higher power so that the healing energies flow through. I recommend using just one, or perhaps two, stones during each healing session for maximum effect. If any of the stones relate to your own health problems, you can use them to give yourself healing so that you are better balanced yourself. Do the chakra healing meditation (pages 92–3) and hold the chosen stone in one of your hands throughout.

Personally I don't advise using crystals and gemstones on their own as a treatment as the energy vibrations are quite subtle. Nothing at all can beat the power and simplicity of hands-on healing, but crystals can be used as an added extra. In this chapter I list the stones that I have personally found most useful when giving healing to a wide variety of animals and birds. You can use pieces of jewellery containing gemstones, as well as individual stones. If you are using a piece of jewellery for healing, it should not be second-hand nor should it belong to anyone else. In the same way your stones should not be used by other people. This is because the vibrational qualities of the stones may be influenced by other people in a way that may not be compatible with your own energies.

Using stones with pet healing

There are several ways to use stones; these are the ways that have worked best for me. You can carry a stone in your pocket or wear one around your neck. If you wear one around your neck, keep it tucked inside your clothing – a pet may grab it or it may dangle in their face. If you have a stone inside your pocket, make sure that it cannot fall out as it could be swallowed. When wearing rings with stones, take care that the pet does not get knocked or injured when you place your hands on or near it to give healing. Stones and crystals can be left in a room where

the pet sleeps, but make sure that they are out of harm's way. When giving healing over the chakras, you can also hold a small stone in your hand to enhance the benefits.

All stones, including those mounted in jewellery, must be cleansed first by leaving them in clean cold water for ten minutes. They should

You can use crystals or gemstones to assist healing by holding them above the body over the chakra energy centres. During a healing session these stones can stimulate and enhance the body's subtle energies. Be very careful in case the animal moves suddenly and never hold stones in front of the face in case of injury.

You can also wear crystals with the relevant property during healing – see pages 142–5 for details.

Important – do not leave stones or crystals lying around. They may get swallowed or cause choking.

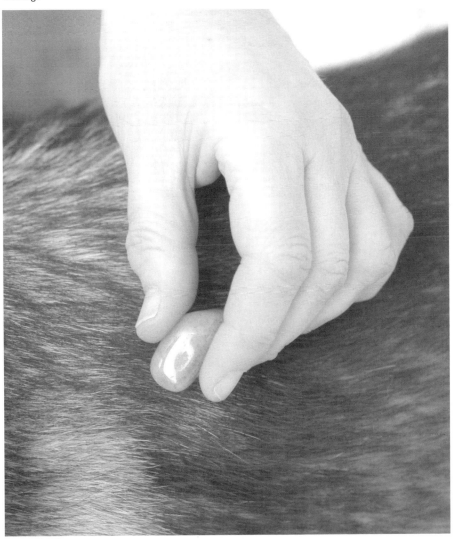

then be left to dry in natural daylight, or even better overnight under a full moon, safely inside the house on a suitable windowsill. If the windowsill is plastic, lay the stones on a piece of unpainted wood. Stones need to be re-cleansed every fortnight to wash out negative energy.

Healing qualities of stones

Agate

This is a stone to use when a sense of happiness, joy and fun is needed. It is also strengthening, and useful with depressed and sad animals, finicky eaters, or pets with digestive problems. Agate is good to use with pets that are used for breeding.

Alexandrite

Alexandrite helps wounds and injuries to heal and tissues to regenerate. Also use it for bereavement, loss of companions, changes in circumstances or routine, and after a house move.

Amber

This has always been my favourite as it is native to my ancestors' home-land in Prussia. Amber is a powerful resinous stone, with energising, balancing and healing properties. It is good for all-round healing, and also for emotional problems. It also has links with the reproductive organs.

Amethyst

Amethyst promotes healing and links with the higher consciousness and sixth sense. It is a lovely gemstone that aids serenity and purification of thought. It is one to use for blessing your pet with peace. You can place it in a fish tank as the stone is also said to reduce infection and parasite invasion. Use it when protection is needed, and it helps disperse negative energy, for example if you live near power cables or phone masts.

Aquamarine

This stone helps with fears and phobias. Use it for healing with nervous and highly-strung pets, especially those from rescue centres.

Azurite

Azurite is linked to the air, so I would use it for chest and breathing problems such as asthma, emphysema, sinusitis and heart conditions.

Bloodstone

Bloodstone is cleansing and purifying. Use it for liver problems and post-viral syndrome. It is also suitable for working and competition dogs and all show animals.

Blue fluorite

I would use this for protection and for shielding a pet from negative energy.

Carnelian

Carnelian strengthens the pet's link to natural spiritual elements. It is useful for depressed pets and those in shock, especially when used over the brachial major or 'key' chakra.

Celestite

This is a balancing stone that promotes vitality and a sense of improved well-being. Use it over the crown chakra.

Citrine

Citrine helps to reduce tension and to clear the mind. It is especially good for treating the solar plexus chakra. It has detoxification properties, so use it over the sacral area for digestive problems and abdominal tumours.

Clear quartz

Clear quartz amplifies healing energy and helps to clear blockages. It is good to use for all health conditions and for stressed or nervous pets.

Diamond

Diamond is the stone for clarity and perfection. Use it to balance the pet on all levels – emotional, mental, physical and spiritual.

Emerald

This is the stone for wisdom, loyalty and trust. I recommend using it if you need to build up a better bond with a pet, or if you want it to understand why you are taking a certain course of action.

Garnet – see Ruby

Jade

Jade is linked to the life force. It helps the heart energy and promotes general vitality.

Jasper

Use this stone for empowerment. Use it over the sacral chakra to help to balance the whole body.

Lapis lazuli

This encourages a pet to express itself and is also linked to hearing. It is useful for lack of confidence or nervousness in pets.

Moonstone

Use this to aid the development of friendship with a pet, to help it to express its inner feelings, and to help you to understand its communication with you.

Onyx

This is for stamina. Use it after illness or surgery. It is suitable for pets with a low immune system, and for those who are in poor condition.

Rose quartz

Rose quartz is the universal healing and clearing crystal and can be used over any chakra. It transmits energy between human and animal. It also enhances peace and tranquillity, and helps with lack of confidence.

Ruby

Ruby is revitalising. Use it after an illness or surgery. After a difficult birth, it can be used for both the baby animal and the mother.

Sapphire

This helps the pet to communicate with us. If it is safe to do so, use sapphire around the throat chakra.

Smoky quartz

It is a classic healing crystal for calmness and grounding. Smoky quartz is helpful for panic and shock, and also with first aid healing.

Snowflake obsidian

Use snowflake obsidian to strengthen an animal in times of change. It relates to the cycle of life and death (and rebirth), and is a good stone to use with very sick pets, and also with those with poor immune systems. It is useful when working with the brachial major (key) chakra.

Snowy quartz

Snowy quartz can be used where there is loneliness or resentment, including rescue animals and those left alone for long periods. It is also good for pets confined to cage- or pen-rest after injury, surgery or illness.

Tiger's eye

This is linked to creativity and courage. It is especially useful before a show or competition for show cats, dogs and rabbits, etc, and for use with working dogs. It is also good for pets who lack confidence and those being introduced to new people or situations.

Using crystals
and gemstones as
a healing aid

Topaz

Topaz is a fertility stone. It is suitable for healing with pets used for breeding.

Tourmaline

This aids compassion and tolerance. Use it with a pet suffering from bereavement or loss of a companion, whether human or animal.

Turquoise

Turquoise relates to mind-body communication. It is another stone to use to help strengthen your bond with a pet.

White fluorite

The properties of white fluorite are used to strengthen an animal's spirit. Use it for pets who have been in rescue or re-homing situations, or who have a history of bad treatment and abuse.

White tourmaline

This stone is the one to use for spiritual enlightenment. It helps promote a sense of well-being at the deepest soul level.

You will notice that several stones or crystals have the same or similar qualities. Use your healing intuition to choose what you feel is right for your pet.

TEDDY AND THE AMBER NECKLACE

I was discussing Teddy, my 18-month-old Snowshoe cat (a Siamese/American shorthair cross-breed), with homeopathic vet Cheryl Sears because he was always hungry. Extensive blood tests had showed up no obvious medical cause for his compulsive obsession with food. Cheryl assessed Teddy as metabolically out-of-balance and asked me what blockages I picked up when giving him healing and which of the chakras in particular felt low in energy. Then she asked me if I had used any gemstones with Teddy. I hadn't, so she said, 'What would you use with him?' Straight away my intuition said amber because this gemstone is particularly balancing and energising, with powerful healing properties. We need to be really vigilant when using gemstones and crystals for healing with pets, especially dogs and cats, because they can take them into their mouths with potentially tragic results, so that evening I took out of my jewellery box an amber necklace – too big for Teddy to try eating. I spread it across my lap and Teddy came to investigate, rubbing against it, and then pushed his head through it. I had to smile as he lay facing me with the beads

145

around his neck. After moving around a bit, Teddy sat facing me, clasping the amber necklace with his paws. He was holding it over his heart chakra. The whole expression on his face then changed – his eyes stared at me and looked like deep, dark pools as he opened his mouth and stuck his tongue out. I had my hand across his sacral chakra and I could feel a huge surge of energy as the vibrational qualities of the amber resonated with his energy field. Teddy then fell asleep for over half an hour and during that time I could feel the energy rhythm settle down. He appeared much brighter after that and the next morning actually left some of his breakfast! The improvements in his eating habits continued over three weeks before I needed to top up the healing again with his amber necklace, and now he is absolutely fine.

9 Pet horoscopes and healing energy

Whatever is born or done this moment, has the qualities of this moment of time.

C.G. Jung

All life on this earth is affected by the influences of the planets and their vibrations. Looking up into the heavens for inspiration and guidance has been something that mankind has done since the beginning of time. The planets and the stars have always been a source of fascination and wonder and have even been worshipped as gods. Our ancestors had advanced knowledge of the solar system. They kept records and maps of the heavens and were able to plot the paths of the planets. Mankind now travels into outer space, researching far-flung galaxies and gathering information to try to unravel the mysteries of these other worlds. Astronomy and astrology have their roots in Babylon, Mesopotamia and originated there with the Chaldeans around 2300BC. These studies later spread to Egypt and Greece. The peoples of Ancient China and India were also skilled astronomers and the Maya of Central America were known to have used astronomy. The earliest records of the zodiac are on the ceiling of a temple in Egypt dating from around 100BC. This zodiac painting uses animals to represent various signs and their qualities, but it was the Ancient Greeks who developed these images into the zodiac as we know it today.

Just like humans, animals need to be emotionally content to be physically in balance. Expression of their feelings is easier to observe in the more socialised domestic pets, such as dogs and cats, but the less complex species, including rabbits, rodents, guinea pigs, hamsters, farm animals, birds and even fish, also express personalities and feelings. Their character traits are usually less distinct, though, compared with those of dogs and cats (and, of course, horses). As each animal is an individual with its own unique character and personality within a species group, so some will be more demonstrative than others, depending on how they feel and their development. Each species has different ways of expressing themselves and some are naturally more vocal than others. Pets will act

true to type according to how their species communicates different emotions. For example, an angry cat will hiss, bite or scratch, an angry dog may bark, growl and bite, and an angry rabbit will throw its dish around or growl and thump the ground. The planets can influence these multi-faceted aspects of their personality and observing some of the astrological characteristics may help us to accept them better for their quirky ways.

SAMANTHA PURRS

When I got a phone call to discuss 'healing for a kitten', I had a mental picture of a cute little baby cat, until the caller, a lady called Liz, explained that it was a rat kitten with a respiratory problem. Samantha was cute, though, and a lovely cinnamon colour. I always take a detailed case history before giving healing and I was intrigued to be told that Samantha had the same birthdate as myself, and was a Cancerian like me (and I was also born in the Chinese horoscope Year of the Rat!). It is much easier, of course, to notice horoscope character traits, and feel the energy influences in dogs and cats than it is in smaller pets, but they are nevertheless also affected by planetary aspects.

Samantha came for healing in a travelling cage with her sister Lucinda. At first I thought that I would give Samantha healing through the cage bars but after a while I took her out and held her. She was very inquisitive and sniffed around my jacket, then for a few seconds nearly disappeared up my sleeve before I retrieved her. Holding Samantha in my hands, I quickly tuned in to the healing energy and within seconds her tiny body started to tremble. Then I heard her purr – just like a cat kitten – a soft ecstatic noise that rats make when they are relaxed and happy. It was a gentle noise that I found very soothing too.

Samantha quickly fell asleep and the sensation in my hands became very soft, as though I was holding a ball of pure light. It was a wonderful experience. Even when Samantha was put back into the cage she did not wake up. As with all my clients, I showed Liz how she could carry on giving some healing to help over the next few days.

Liz placed her hands just like I showed her and reported back a week later. She told me that Samantha always made the purring noise as soon as the healing began. Liz now gives healing to both rats on a regular basis just because they are so responsive and obviously enjoy it. And of course this helps on a preventative basis too.

The universal connection

Everything in the universe is connected – our earth, the life on it and the solar system. All of these components are related to each other, and the forces of the planets influence our pets emotionally as well as physically.

The word horoscope comes from the words *hora*, meaning the hour, and *skopos*, meaning to observe. By observing when our pets were born, we can gain some insight into the influences of cosmic energy and how that can affect the overall energy field of the individual and the healing responses as well. The word zodiac comes from the Ancient Greek word *zodiskos*, meaning a circle of animals. The science of studying the influences of the cosmic forces on the affairs of the earth and its life forms is called astrology.

Linking healing to astrology

I find astrology fascinating from a healing point of view because the planets vibrate with an energy and each is different. These vibrations influence the life force energy rhythm and flow in all living things. When giving healing to pets, I find that I can frequently feel the difference in these energy patterns. This is much easier to pick up in the bigger animals, such as cats and dogs. The smaller the animal, the more subtle the energy. The first time that I noticed this phenomenon was a few years ago when giving healing to two Leonberger dogs, Brewin and Chewy. I detected that the feel and strength of the rhythm was completely different in the two dogs, even though they were a similar age and the same breed and their problems were both joint-related. The client who has them, Pam, is an astrologer, and she asked me to describe the two dogs' energy patterns. With Chewy, I described a very slow and strong rhythm. When I had my hands on him, I felt as though I was going into a meditation. With Brewin, the flow of energy felt much quicker but not as strong as with Chewy. Pam told me that what I was picking up was a very accurate description of the type of resonance associated with their ruling planets. Chewy is a Pisces and Brewin a Virgo. Chewy always responded in a dreamy Piscean way to the healing (Pam would always say that he was 'off with the fairies' as soon as I touched him), while Brewin was a typical Virgo in that initially he would find it difficult to relax into the sessions and let himself go.

149

Blending energies in harmony

Our own energies need to blend with our pet's energies for harmony and to help us adapt to their natures, and vice versa. Living in close proximity to humans encourages our pets to make their feelings known and this helps us to see more of their individual personality. Animal behaviour can follow a pattern within a species and knowing what characteristics the planets influence can also help us to understand them better.

All the planets represent energy forces within our charts and animals are very sensitive to these forces. Animal behaviour is reflected by certain planetary action as the planets move around the universe in relation to one another. We know that all the world is influenced in some way too, for example the moon has a gravitational pull on the tides. Both humans and animals are known to be influenced by phases of the moon, with a rise in disturbed behaviour during a full moon period and a reduction in such behaviour during the first and last quarters. Researchers at Leeds University in the UK have been able to confirm that behaviour is dramatically affected during the period following a full moon. They identified a link between this lunar phase and human well-being, with an increase in the number of visits made to the family doctor for six days just after a full moon. Scientists now believe this is due to the gravitational pull on our bodies as we are made mostly of water, as are all mammals, including our cats, dogs, rabbits, etc. I have certainly noticed my own pets are much more active at this time and I find that tapping into healing energy during this phase can be much more powerful too. The moon influences the fluid in a body and this includes the fluid in the brain and in the cells. So we can see it has a huge influence not just on behaviour but on chemical constituents. The sun planetary aspects influence the cerebellum part of the brain, responsible for functions including the senses, memory and emotions. The other planets influence the organs with which they have a vibrational affinity, and therefore are said to rule them. The chakras too have an influence on certain organs in their vicinity, so we can see how cosmic and physical energies are all interrelated in a very complex way. We need to take this into account when dealing with illness and disorder.

All life on this earth, including humans and animals, is affected in some way by the influences of the planets and their vibrations.

Feeling the energy

If you know two animals that have different birth signs, try putting your hands on them and seeing if you can pick up the variation in energy flow. Check out what parts of the body the signs rule (see below) and you may notice a variation with the chakras governing those areas too. As you practise giving healing, this is something that you should become more skilled in sensing. The different planet energies are listed under each zodiac section. To detect energy flow as influenced by the planets, it is better to place your hands gently on larger pets, such as cats, dogs or rabbits, at a time when they are resting or asleep so that you are not distracted by their body movements.

The signs

There are twelve signs of the zodiac and as the sun circulates through the sky it passes through each one of them in turn. For this reason they are often called 'sun signs'. The information given below is a brief general overview of the character influences of each sign, their dates, associated colour and type of energy the planet vibrates with. For an accurate birth chart, it's best to consult an astrologer, giving them the pet's exact time, place and date of birth. The environment the pet is kept in and how it was raised and socialised will also play a significant role in the pet's expression of its character and development. All signs have both positive and negative characteristics and pets can demonstrate one more than another. The age of the pet also needs to be taken into consideration as personalities and energies develop as the animal gets older and wiser.

Our own birth sign is also relevant regarding our pets because it will influence how we relate to other signs. Our compatibility with our pets will play a role in how we view them and tolerate their behaviour. The type of pet also needs to be taken into account when interpreting the horoscope. It is essential to know exactly what the best lifestyle is for the type of pet, so it is important to seek specialist advice from a veterinarian. Some species' natural instinct is to be solitary and territorial, and some will fight with each other unless they are neutered. Other animals are very sociable and need to be in pairs or groups.

What if you aren't sure when your pet was born? A quick glance through the character descriptions below should give you a clue. Remember that a mix of planets influence our pets, depending on their aspects to each other at the exact time of birth (the same as with

151

humans), so your pet may have character traits from more than one birth sign.

The twelve signs of the zodiac are divided into four elements - air, water, fire and earth. These reflect the emotional and personality traits which the signs influence. Generally air signs are sociable charmers, and are very expressive. Water signs tend to live in their emotions and can be dreamy. Fire signs are explosive, adventurous and high-spirited, while earth signs are solid, dependable, grounded types.

The signs are further grouped together to define their qualities. Aries, Cancer, Libra and Capricorn are Cardinal signs, which means that these individuals tend to be restless and want to initiate change. Taurus, Leo, Scorpio and Aquarius are Fixed signs, and those born under them are inclined to be very set in their ways. Gemini, Virgo, Sagittarius and Pisces are Mutable signs and are easily bored, always waiting for something different to happen.

Aries (March 21–April 20)

- The Ram
- Fire
- Planetary ruler: Mars
- Colour: red
- Parts of the body: head and face, muscular system
- Energy vibration: strong and driving, fast

Individuals under the influence of Aries will have high-focused energy, often in short bursts. The energy weakens as they get older. When giving healing to this group, expect the energy you pick up to feel quick, active and strong. I have found that even if the pet is very sick, the energy will feel stronger than I would expect. Aries pets are vibrant and become energised quickly and therefore can respond quickly to healing.

The positive energy pet is active, independent, courageous, enthusiastic, adventurous and confident. The negative energy pet is impulsive, impatient, self-centred, over-the-top, selfish and quick-tempered.

Taurus (April 21–May 20)

- The Bull
- Earth
- Planetary ruler: Venus
- Colour: blue and pink

- Parts of the body: neck and throat, skin
- Energy vibration: slow, fixed and steady

Animals in the house of Taurus will have a steady, regular energy flow and it can often be difficult to effect a change in the rhythm. Patience and persistence is needed when giving healing to these individuals to connect with their energy type, and they can be slower to respond. The throat chakra may easily become blocked. Taurus is ruled by Venus, so will enjoy being the centre of attention, including being given regular healing for the feel-good factor it produces.

The positive energy pet is faithful, stable, reliable, dependable, predictable and patient. The negative energy pet is stubborn, possessive, obsessive, greedy and inflexible.

Gemini (May 21– June 20)

- The Twins
- Air
- Planetary ruler: Mercury
- Colour: dark silver
- Parts of the body: paws, forelimbs, nervous system, lungs
- Energy vibration: quick, light, changeable

Animals born under the erratic energy of Mercury will have highly charged senses and so when receiving healing they are usually very sensitive to the sensations. The volatile energy means that these individuals have very quick nervous energy too. Treatment time may need to be adjusted accordingly and the energy flow can rebalance quickly. The auras of these pets will usually feel very delicate and soft.

The positive energy pet is amusing, communicative, spontaneous, clever, versatile and curious. The negative energy pet is fickle, restless, flighty, inconsistent, noisy and mischievous.

Cancer (June 21–July 23)

- The Crab
- Water
- Planetary ruler: the Moon
- Colour: pale silver
- Parts of the body: stomach, mammary glands
- Energy vibration: fluid, gentle and comforting

153

Cancerians are emotionally sensitive creatures and their heart chakra can easily become blocked. The energy flow of these pets should feel strong and rhythmical and the magnetic field can often draw the healer's hand inwards. I would expect a very powerful surge of energy to be experienced at the time of a full moon. For chronically sick Cancerian pets, give them healing at this time especially. Cancer moods are particularly influenced by the phases and vibrations of the moon as it is the ruling planet.

The positive energy pet is sensitive, loyal, sympathetic, intuitive, protective and maternal. The negative energy pet is moody, shy, over-emotional, clingy, hypersensitive and irritable.

Leo (July 23–August 22)

- The Lion
- Fire
- Planetary ruler: the Sun
- Colour: gold and scarlet
- Parts of the body: heart, spine and back
- Energy vibration: strong, fixed, fiery

I always expect the energy of Leo pets to be flowing in a fairly positive fashion, even if the animal is unwell. After healing I would aim for the energy flow to be as powerful as possible. These are centre-stage individuals who like attention so they should love the sensation of the healing. It is important to keep the heart chakra of a Leo pet open and flowing strongly.

The positive energy pet is affectionate, brave, the life and soul of the party, dramatic and protective. The negative energy pet is domineering, loud, uncompromising, flamboyant and intense.

Virgo (August 24–September 23)

- The Maiden
- Earth
- Planetary ruler: Mercury
- Colour: grey and navy
- Parts of the body: front paws, nervous system, solar plexus, intestines
- Energy vibration: precise, quick

Animals born under this sign can be very anxious types, so when giving healing take some time to reassure them first. The natural rhythm of

their energy field can appear to be very fast because the energy vibration of Mercury is quick and this will influence our pet. Like Gemini pets who are also ruled by Mercury, they will be sensitive to the healing energy, feeling the changes and responses easily. The Virgo energy is an anxious energy too and the solar plexus chakra is important to give healing over.

The positive energy pet is caring, loyal, precise, anxious to please and well groomed. The negative energy pet is fussy, detached, temperamental, unfriendly and edgy.

Libra (September 24–October 23)

- The Scales
- Air
- Planetary ruler: Venus
- Colour: blue and pink
- Parts of the body: kidneys, lower back, lymph
- Energy vibration: balanced, calm

It is very important for the energy flow of the Libran to be always in balance, like their symbol the scales. Always check the root chakra of these pets to keep them grounded. When in balance, Librans have a soothing aura about them and radiate pleasing energy to everyone around them. Being in their presence is calming and the Libran pet will enjoy drifting off to sleep during healing sessions. Venus, which rules Libra, is the planet of love and beauty so expect these pets especially to want lots of love.

The positive energy pet is charming, easy-going, sociable, even-tempered, co-operative and relaxed. The negative energy pet is manipulative, devious, shallow, lazy and indecisive.

Scorpio (October 24–November 22)

- The Scorpion
- Water
- Planetary ruler: Pluto
- Colour: black
- Parts of the body: reproductive organs, bladder, bowel
- Energy vibration: deep, powerful, steady, strong

This is an emotional water sign so these pets will respond deeply to healing energy and the potential to release emotional blockages. The sensation of their energy field will often feel turbulent and the

crown chakra is one to check with these individuals. Scorpio energy runs deep and is very intense. This means they can pick up your thought energy and moods. The Pluto influence means they like to be in charge too.

The positive energy pet is focused, competitive, resourceful, deep thinking, intense and independent. The negative energy pet is sly, jealous, resentful, spiteful, stubborn and moody.

Sagittarius (November 23–December 21)

- The Archer
- Fire
- Planetary ruler: Jupiter
- Colour: purple
- Parts of the body: liver, hips and thighs
- Energy vibration: fiery, excessive energy

These pets may find it difficult to concentrate on letting go and fidget when you try to give them healing. However, once they get the hang of it, they will love it and be responsive. They are free spirits and their energy field needs to fly high for them to feel really in balance and at peace. The Sagittarius energy level is higher than those of the other fire signs and can be a bit over-the-top. Their active Jupiter energy means they need to move about a lot and this influences their emotional and physical health.

The positive energy pet is persistent, athletic, sociable, fearless, spirited and adventurous. The negative energy pet is quarrelsome, careless, obstinate, restless and temperamental.

Capricorn (December 22–January 20)

- The Goat
- Earth
- Planetary ruler: Saturn
- Colour: grey and black
- Parts of the body: bones, skin and knees
- Energy vibration: purposeful, strong, steady

The energy of this sign is latent which means that in the young it will be slow and weak, getting stronger as the pet gets older. Saturn influences a change in more upbeat energy as the animal ages. So when giving

healing expect to achieve a stronger flow of energy the older the animal is. If this energy field gets out of rhythm, the pet will really feel out of sorts as the flow needs to be regular and constant. The energy vibration of Saturn is purposeful and so these individuals will be determined and steadfast.

The positive energy pet is patient, cautious, sure-footed, responsible and intelligent. The negative energy pet is intolerant, reclusive, unforgiving, inhibited and manipulative.

Aquarius (January 21–February 19)

- The Water Carrier
- Air
- Planetary ruler: Uranus
- Colour: electric blue
- Parts of the body: circulation, lower limbs, ankles
- Energy vibration: erratic, volatile, unpredictable

Placing your healing hands on these pets can be a 'live wire' experience and the tingle sensation of the healing energy can often feel like little electric shocks. As the natural energy is quite volatile, the Aquarius pet should respond quickly to changes through any healing energy being offered. The energy can have a real buzz to it. Uranus is not a steady planet and is always changing, so Aquarian pets are always shifting around and changing direction in response to their influential planet.

The positive energy pet is intuitive, good natured, inventive, curious and independent. The negative energy pet is stubborn, rebellious, insecure, eccentric, erratic and inattentive.

Pisces (February 20–March 20)

- The Fish
- Water
- Planetary ruler: Neptune
- Colour: sea green
- Parts of the body: feet and lymphatic system
- Energy vibration: sensitive, weak, slow

Neptune rules the sea and I find the energy of the Piscean pet moves like waves breaking against the shore. This energy has a strong rhythm with a loud amplitude. The mystical quality makes for a deep connection and

these animals frequently go into a trance-like state with healing as they tune into the universe and the spiritual world. The Neptune influence means that telepathy comes easily to these pets and they have a particularly strong ability to be healers both of other animals and their human friends. They often have a tendency to be dreamy and 'other worldly'.

The positive energy pet is gentle, intuitive, unassuming, emotional, sympathetic and psychic. The negative energy pet is changeable, irrational, depressive, timid and careless.

10 When it's time to let go

What is life? It is the flash of a firefly in the night. It is the breath of the buffalo in the winter time. It is the shadow which runs across the grass and loses itself in the sunset.

Crowfoot, Chief of the Blackfoot Nation

Often my work as a healer involves helping terminally ill pets at the end of their physical life journey, which may also mean helping the distraught human come to terms with their companion's condition. It is never easy to let go and say goodbye but the way that I look at it when faced with the same decision is that the love they gave me was so great, so pure and so unconditional, that my love must be stronger than my grief and impending sense of loss. My emotional pain is less important than the pet's welfare, for there must be no torment for them at the end of their life if I can help it. Their reward for befriending me and healing me whenever I needed it must be my mercy. All pets are special, but we build a stronger bond with some than with others. Each relationship is, however, equally rewarding and each pet teaches us something new, helps us to grow spiritually as we go through the difficult process of life, and is our healer whenever we need it.

People sometimes ask me why my own pets get sick or die. 'If you are a healer, why can't you fix them?' they say. Well, I do give all my animals healing frequently and if I wasn't doing that they wouldn't be as well as they possibly can be. However, healing it is not going to change an individual's destiny or make something last forever. I often read in the papers of some scientist or other saying that a new invention or drug will mean that we or our pets could live for hundreds of years. I don't believe that will ever be so, because I believe that this life is a learning zone and that our real world is to come. There is absolutely no point in us being here for hundreds of years, and we need to look to whether we are leading a healing life today because that is our future for the next stage of our spiritual development.

There is much in the news now about animal cloning, with much interest from people who want to invest in this process so that when

their pet dies they can have a replica. Well, let's make no mistake – cloning does *not* give us a replica pet. Cloning will produce an animal that is genetically identical, but it will not be born with the same experiences of life or have the same personality, and it may not even look the same. That was unique to the previous animal. Moreover, in the years that we shared with them we will have developed and changed too. Our pet responded to that joint acquaintance and that was in part what shaped its character, so therefore no relationship can ever be the same again. Each relationship with an animal is unique and enriching, and goes to shape our own character too. Furthermore, cloning involves animal experimentation and many suffer and die in the process. Is that what our pets would want of us? Wouldn't our beloved pet surely ask of us that we reach out our healing hand to a paw, claw or hoof that needs the home that they have vacated?

Healing for the terminally ill pet

Healing given to the terminally ill pet is very potent and assists the transition from this life, easing the spiritual journey. This is the most precious gift of healing – the mind/body/spirit preparation for the final journey from earth. In my experience, healing always gives a feeling of peace to terminally ill animals and strengthens the pet's spiritual connection. The endorphins released through healing are known to have an effect like morphine, thereby helping with pain relief and also improving mental well-being. In these circumstances healing can be given several times a day and even given when the vet is performing euthanasia.

I can sympathise with the feelings of being emotionally and physically drained at these times, but if you are looking after a very sick animal, try to give healing as often as you possibly can – even if it is just for a few minutes. The connection made will help you both. Connecting with your beloved pet in this way should leave you feeling stronger because you will both be joined in another dimension as the healing flows and you are jointly bathed in a blessing. This is also a time to call in the professional healer if you are very troubled and upset, or ask a sympathetic friend to help you.

After your pet has passed away, keep sending out your thoughts of love: remember that your pet will exist as a spark of the universal life force for eternity.

ALAN

I have a very soft spot for bunnies, having lived with several of them over the years, and Alan was as cute as any I've come across. He was grey and white with floppy ears like a lop. Sue, a vet nurse, was his loving care-giver and had looked after Alan since he was three weeks old. He was now six and a half years of age. Sue hand-raised him when he was brought into the veterinary hospital suffering with coccidiosis, and then had taken him home to be her very special pet. Coccidia are common parasites in rabbits, invisible to the naked eye, which can attack the liver or intestines, and infection with coccidia must be treated urgently by a vet. Under Sue's loving care, Alan had a life of luxury, living in the house with her other pets and freedom to go in the garden. For years all had been well until he suddenly started to show digestive problems. Although he was on medication, things didn't look very hopeful.

Sue placed Alan onto my lap and I laid my hands either side of his back and began giving him healing. Instantly he settled and became sleepy, the back of his neck quivering in pleasure. The solar plexus chakra was, I noticed, depleted. The aura in this area looked very weak too. Sue said that it confirmed what she already knew – that Alan had a large malignant tumour in his intestines. The next communication from Alan was very poignant. He told me he was ready to go, but was hanging on because he loved Sue so much and was concerned for her. The soft feeling then between my hands as I held him is almost impossible to describe. I felt as though he was flying, that he had left his body to experience the deep peace that was there for eternity. I could see rainbow colours between my hands and Sue could see them too. I felt that if he could, Alan would have slipped away there and then. He didn't, of course, and Sue had the nightmare of visiting the vet the following day to have Alan put to sleep.

I strongly felt that another pet was round the corner for Sue and that evening the telephone rang – she had been offered a young Belgian hare. Sue collected it and loves it very much, already beginning a special new relationship with him. Alan's story is a very good example of how beneficial healing is for the terminally ill pet in offering tremendous peace for both animal and human at this traumatic time.

Sue called the hare Dennis and you can see him in the photo on page 12.

Client experiences

Clients often tell me of the special experiences they have when they use healing energy for the terminally ill. I would like to tell you a very special story. Maralyn had a very close bond with her golden labrador dog, Bertie, whom she had had from a puppy. When Bertie was ten and Maralyn was in her forties, they both shared the trauma and shock of developing cancer.

Maralyn came to me for healing after her breast cancer was operated on. When she discovered that I treated animals, she started bringing Bertie along for help with his stiff joints. Just as Maralyn's cancer returned, Bertie developed cancer in some lymph nodes near the liver and, after surgery to remove them, his long-term prognosis was not good. A combination of healing and homeopathy gave the dog another 18 months to support Maralyn as her condition worsened. She rang me the day he died and told me how special it had been, how she had given him healing and felt the life force energies gathering to leave the body. He was very peaceful, she said, but the most wonderful thing had happened. After the vet had declared him clinically dead, Maralyn sent a thought out saying she hoped her dog was at peace and happy – suddenly Bertie's tail gave not one, but two big wags. The vet said that she had never seen anything like it. Earlier in this book I explained how thought becomes living energy, which is picked up by our pets. Bertie was still there in energy form, even though he had left his body. Maralyn had her answer and she joined her beloved dog a few months later.

Grief and bereavement

The death of a much loved pet can be a truly devastating time. The demise of a companion animal means the end of a period in our lives and can leave us with feelings of grief, panic and fear as we face the world an emptier place. If the pet was elderly, then death is something that we can usually accept as part of the ageing process. However, when a young animal is taken suddenly from us, the shock can be very difficult to come to terms with and we agonise over the years that we planned to share but are now lost forever. Accidents, disease or injury can all take their toll. Dealing with the demise of a pet meeting a sudden and violent end is traumatising and debilitating for us. At these times I advise that people have some healing for themselves to help them find some sense of peace.

The pet may be stolen or disappear, and then the grief cannot be resolved and is made worse by endless worry and hoping against hope that the animal will return to our lives. If still alive, the pet will also be missing us; knowing that makes it so very hard to cope with.

Send out healing thoughts several times a day. If you have anything belonging to the pet, hold it to help you tune in. With so many couples today splitting up, another reason for grief can be because companion animals have been taken to live with another person. Not being in a relationship with the animal any more is equally depressing and can result in feelings of deep grief for both human and pet. Whenever I get a letter from someone describing the death or loss of a very dear companion animal, I can always sympathise with their sentiments. This is a selection of some of the words people have used to describe the experience to me:

- 'Even now, many months after our parting, I mourn her daily, some days being easier to bear than others, some days triggering off a precious memory which brings the sense of loss back as strongly as ever.'

- 'It was a beautiful sunny day today, yet it was all so meaningless because he was not with me. The flattened patch in the flower bed where he used to lie and watch me pottering around is all I have left now.'

- 'I miss his vibrancy and his love.'

All of these words will strike a chord in the hearts of those who have suffered with grief for the loss of a pet. People expect humans to feel distraught when a close friend or relative dies and so give them sympathy and make allowances. However, when it comes to the death of a pet many people are quite insensitive and intolerant, so we often hide our grief and sense of loss from the world around us. When we experience grieving for a pet we often feel guilty because it was 'just an animal'. However, the pet we have lost was not just an animal – it was part of our soul energy, a reflection of our love and an extension of all that we are and have experienced while they were in our care. We feel that everything has been taken away when they left. That is why the hole in our heart feels so huge, why the pain hurts so much, why we feel so empty. But in reality nothing has been taken away by the process we call death, other than the physical body of the animal. We reflected our love onto them, and they reflected their love to us. We still have that within

163

us; it is permanently added to our life force, and the memories we have are what have helped make us the person that we are today.

Symptoms of pet grief

The process of grief produces classical post-traumatic stress disorder symptoms. These include not being able to sleep, nightmares, depression, lack of appetite and reluctance to eat, over-eating (if the grief has affected the hormone system, this may lead to a state of obesity), mood swings, and a lack of interest in life in general. We need to remember at these times that an animal life is just as valid as any other type of life and should be respected for the role it has played in the global picture, the jigsaw of the complex interaction of all energies.

During the pet bereavement process, we may be shocked by the intense feelings that come over us, not just sadness, but waves of deep inner turmoil that often create a feeling of tightness or aching in the chest area. This is because the heart chakra is working overtime to help balance us at these times. It is a good time to practise the chakra meditation on pages 92–3 to help keep these energy centres open and linking strongly to each other.

Guilt is common during the grieving process. We feel that we should have done more; we agonise about whether we made the right decisions; we remember all the times that we were impatient or came home late. However, we should remember that we did our best at the time. We can all look back and wish that we had done things differently, but we can learn from our mistakes. Out pets loved us so much, so unconditionally, that they forgave us everything; we just need to forgive ourselves so that we can offer that love again, not least of all to ourselves. The lyricist Adam Duratz sang, 'The price of a memory is the memory of the sorrow it brings.' The sorrow is not being able to enjoy the day-to-day relationship any more, but the memory of that rapport we had is joyous and priceless.

Animals who grieve

Companion animals also suffer from bereavement. This may be grief for another animal or for a human who is no longer part of their lives. Animals in rescue centres can also grieve for a previous home if the reason for leaving it was not abuse-related. Relationships break up, health or money problems occur, people have to go into hospital or into care, people die – all these are reasons why animals end up losing their homes. Animals can suffer from the same symptoms of grief that affect humans, including depression, eating disorders and shock-related illnesses. But animals cannot cry or talk, like people can, to help release the grief. This is a role that healing plays very well in helping the pet to let go.

HARRY LETS GO OF HIS PAINFUL MEMORIES

Harry, a four-year-old silver tabby British shorthair cat, was referred to my colleague, veterinary physiotherapist Amanda Sutton, as he was stiff and limping. Two years previously Harry had run across the road outside his house with his brother, who had been knocked down and killed. Harry had come home in a very traumatised condition, but the vet found no real injuries on him and prescribed rest. Harry had never been the same since that day, becoming very withdrawn, but numerous veterinary examinations found nothing physically wrong with him. As time went on, however, Harry got stiffer in his walk, which was why he was sent to the physiotherapist. She was disturbed to find Harry dull and lethargic, with abnormal body tone, and suspected that he was still in shock after his accident, even though it had happened a long time ago.

The care-giver thought that it would be a good idea for the cat to have some healing first and the vet agreed. As soon as I touched Harry, I could feel lots of tears inside him and grief for his brother – all feelings he could not express or release. He was very much emotionally blocked and this disturbed energy started to come away very quickly. He pushed his body into my hands and looked into my eyes as if to say, 'At last someone has heard me.' Harry had witnessed his brother's death and the trauma was still very much in his system. After a while, the healing made Harry feel very calm and he lay across my lap, his eyes closed in peace, then he slept.

Caroline, his care-giver, was astonished the next day to find a lively, bright-eyed Harry trotting around the house. She was even more surprised when he went into the guest bedroom. It was where he used to sleep with his brother and a room he had refused to go in since the tragic accident two years earlier. He had a good look round at everything and sniffed the place where he used to sleep as if to say, 'It's okay now, I'm at peace.'

Harry came to see Amanda again a few days later and she was pleased to find that the improvement after the healing session now meant she was able to release some muscle spasms. Harry never looked back and is full of energy and playful again now. 'Just like he used to be before that terrible day,' says Caroline.

In my experience as a healer, animals can grieve for many years for another animal, wondering where it is and what happened to it. This type of grief can respond very well to healing. Usually in my experience one or two sessions of healing will release the emotionally disturbed energy created by the pet's grief. It is for this reason that when one of my pets dies or is put to sleep I always let the others see the body. Animals understand physical death, so this helps prevent them from looking for the deceased pet, even though they will still miss its company. If an animal has gone missing or pets have been split up due to family circumstances, then healing can help those grieving release the bottled-up emotion. In these circumstances consider asking for professional help because if you are upset or very stressed then the healing connection will not be very strong.

Where does a pet go when it dies?

Most people, when faced with the death of a much loved companion animal, desperately want to know that it goes on to another life – that death of the physical body is not the end. Some people have told me that they are afraid that animals are too low in the scheme of things to have an afterlife, and that it is only for humans. All life comes from the one source of energy and that does not differentiate or discriminate about returning to it when the physical life ends. When a pet passes away from this world the inner individual spark of life that is the sum total of all its energies leaves and returns to the great source in the universe from where it came. Where is that? It's my opinion that no one has the full answer as to what happens next. Mankind is not yet ready for that knowledge or capable of comprehending it, but can get a glimpse, I believe, by working with healing energy. The words of Christopher Fry sum it up for me when he says, 'Between our birth and our death we may touch understanding as a moth brushes a window with its wing.'

Energy, including the life force energy of all living creatures, cannot be destroyed, but only converted from one form to another. Because of my experiences as a healer, I know there is another life and that animals go there too. I have given healing to many animals when they have died and on each occasion I have felt the life force leave the body. It has always been a most bizarre yet spiritually uplifting experience. As I hold these animals, I have always felt the sensations of the spark of life leaving the body – the soul energy.

The first time that this happened to me was with a very sick bunny called Marmalade about 30 years ago. I had my hands on her giving

healing as the vet was putting her to sleep and received what felt like an electric shock throughout my body. My arms flew away from Marmalade so strongly that I was thrown sideways. 'What on earth was that?' I asked the vet, but he didn't seem to know what I was talking about. I just knew that the experience was something to do with Marmalade's soul leaving her body. I think it was so marked on that occasion because it was a new experience and also to let me know that this was something that I should look out for – a sort of 'wake-up call'.

Another special and profound experience happened to me when I held an elderly dog called Toby as he died. I felt a rhythmical drumming in the fingers of my left hand, which was over his shoulder where there is a major chakra. The drumming sensation was spinning like a wheel and I could feel many layers to this movement. It rose to a crescendo then flew outwards into the air. At that point I knew that Toby had truly left the body he had borrowed for his life on this earth. 'He's gone now,' I said to the vet, and he confirmed that that point had been the actual time of clinical death.

As time has gone by and I've been with many animals in the same circumstances, I have experienced something similar every time. It confirms to me that the life force, or soul, leaves to go elsewhere and joins the sum total of the universal cosmic energy. The sceptical can point to these examples and say it was imagination. My advice is to believe what your heart tells you is right – be guided by your own inner knowledge. Sceptics who have closed minds and hearts can take away our comfort and our pleasure if we allow them to. An open mind leads us to new discoveries and new horizons.

In the sunshine

The death of a very special pet can only be understood by someone who has also suffered such an intense sense of loss. I have often been present to give healing to pets when they have been put to sleep by the vet and I am always reminded at these times of my own losses. The most recent was one of my cats, Floyd, who had an incurable disease. I knew that losing him would be devastating, but I was unprepared for the intensity of the hurting. I suppose it hurt so much because I loved him so much – and still do. Six months after that dreadful day when he passed away, I was sitting in the garden watching the bees buzzing round the flowers. I remembered how Floyd would have jumped at my ankles as I walked past and how he hid in the middle of the hosta plants with only the tip

of his nose showing, thinking about some new mischief. The sun shone, yet it was not the golden glow of warmth and happiness for me that day – it was just a light in the sky.

Going into the house, my eyes fell on a CD that a client had given me a couple of days before. I decided to play it to cheer myself up and put the music system onto random play. A song started and the words grabbed my attention. I knew they had a message for me: 'Love of my life, where are you now on this earth… On a white horse we would ride like the wind… we share the moon and the stars for all eternity, the road is long and I am with you never ending, we're walking along in the sunshine.' I looked out of the window as the song played and the sunshine lit up the places where Floyd loved to be in the garden. The song had reminded me that he was with me still, walking in the sunshine. The bit about the horse was particularly significant and poignant because when Floyd was very ill I whispered in his ear that one day we would gallop together through the sky on a horse. Floyd had purred and nuzzled my ear in approval. I know that one day when it is my time to leave this earth, I will meet him again and the many other animals I've given healing to that are no longer with us physically.

An hour later, I had a phone call from a client, Michael, whose dog Ygrec, a large black labrador, I had been giving healing to for about three years. Ygrec was already elderly when I met him and feeling the discomfort of arthritis. After a couple of years, he had his spleen removed due to a malignant tumour, then the cancer spread to his stomach. The call that came that day confirmed that Ygrec was ready to go and a vet had been sent for. I joined Ygrec and Michael in their garden where they were sitting on a rug under the trees. Ygrec looked very tired and although he was pleased to see me and wagged his tail furiously, he didn't get up. The vet arrived and I laid my hands onto the dog's shoulder to begin the healing and said a few words to honour his life and the joy he had brought to the family he lived with. As the vet gave the injection, the bells from the village church suddenly started to peal (there was a wedding taking place), and it seemed the most fitting goodbye. Ygrec slipped away very quickly, with the bells still playing celebratory music for the new life beginning in the church and the old life ending here in the garden. On the way home I played 'In the Sunshine' again and I knew that Ygrec would be nodding his wise old head as I sang along to the words.

The CD had been given to me by Terry Sullivan, the drummer and percussionist from the band Renaissance, when I gave healing to his cat Tilly who had cancer. The words of this song are printed here – and I hope that anyone who has lost a pet will find as much comfort in them as I have.

In the sunshine

Love of my life
Where are you now on this earth
Safe and secure on the deep ocean floor
You were always there
You're on my mind
Longing for you in my life
On a white horse we would ride like the wind
All the loving times
All my life and emotion
Always there calling to me
Any time reach out and I'll be there

And though we're far apart
We'll always have our love
We'll always be the same
So look into the sky
We share the moon and stars
For all eternity
The road is long and I am with you never ending
We're walking along in the sunshine

Here in my heart floating in a gondola of dreams
You will appear as the mist disappears
I will hear our song
When you are gone
To a place beyond the sun
Silence is heard all the wondrous words
You're the only one
All my love all my emotion
Always there calling to me
Any time reach out and I'll be there

And though we're far apart
We'll always have our love
We'll always be the same
So look into the sky
We share the moon and stars
For all eternity
The road is long and I am with you never ending
We're walking along in the sunshine

Everything physical comes to an end, a process that we call death. This end includes the animals, birds, insects, wildlife, creatures of the sea and all the pets that share our lives. It is a difficult challenge to accept the loss of a beloved companion and the grief is as intense as if it were a member of our own family – and, of course, a pet is part of our family group. The memories and the energy of the pet we have lost are permanently there for us to keep inside us always and the shared experience has shaped us and made us what we are today. The life force of the pet cannot be destroyed and lives on in the universal energy. Giving healing strengthens the eternal bond between us and our beloved pets.

11 Using a healer to help your pet

All things are born of the unborn, and from this unity of life flows the brotherhood and compassion for all creatures.

Buddha

There can be times when, for one reason or another, you may wish to call upon the services of a registered healer to give a treatment to your pet. If the pet is very ill, for example, you may be too upset to channel the healing effectively, or you may be going through a tough time and feel depleted. When we are tense or unhappy, the animal picks up on our energy vibes, which affects them adversely, so they worry about us too much to relax into the healing. A professional healer will be detached from the problems and be able to give healing to both human and pet to clear the shared energy. Another reason to call in help is that you may not be confident enough in your own healing abilities to deal with a particular condition, or you may just wish to have the support of an experienced healer. A change in routine affecting the pet is often a good time to consider using a healer. This can include a house move, breakdown of a relationship, someone going away, a bereavement (animal or human), a new addition to the family (such as a baby or a new pet), or the pet having recently arrived from a re-homing centre. Healing helps animals to deal with the disturbed emotional energy, which in the long term can lead to physical and/or behavioural problems.

People have also asked me to give healing to a much loved pet for no other reason than they believe in the general therapeutic benefit of healing working on a preventative level. The idea is that by keeping the energies balanced, pets will have a stronger immune system, and any illnesses or injuries will resolve more quickly. Basically you can use a healer for any condition that your pet has a problem with. Often I'm asked to give healing when everything else has failed.

Registered animal healers in the UK work within the 1966 Veterinary Act and will seek approval from the vet before they give

healing. The Royal College of Veterinary Surgeons (RCVS) has stated that it raises no objection to healing by the laying on of hands, provided that a veterinarian has been consulted first. I was pleased that after having read my first book *Healing for Horses*, a spokesperson for the RCVS wrote that they did not consider that a horse would come to any harm from the methods I described. The methods outlined in this book are very similar. Other parts of the world have their own rules and laws regarding healers and your vet can advise you on this. If you are interested in having healing for your pet, mention this to your vet as many have an open mind about such things nowadays and may even know of a reputable healer to refer you to. It is important to remember that healers do not make a diagnosis or prescribe anything, nor will they make any promises as to the benefits of healing.

The pet's problems

Talk to the healer about the nature of your pet's problem and what diagnosis the vet has made. Some vets also like feedback about how the healing treatments progress. It is essential to tell the healer if the animal can be aggressive with people, has ever attacked or bitten anyone, or is extremely nervous with strangers. In these cases distant healing is usually the best option for safety reasons and to keep stress to the pet to a minimum. Some pets prefer being in the presence of women to men, or vice versa, so this needs to be taken into consideration when making your choice of healer. It is unfair and stressful to transport an animal unnecessarily that is very sick or terminally ill. In these situations, consider asking for distant healing to be sent (see page 134).

It is important to be clear about how healing can benefit your pet and this needs to be discussed with the healer. Healing works on a general level to rebalance the energy field so that the animal can function better. Often this means that physical or emotional problems, or both, improve or even disappear, but no promises of a cure or recovery are ever given. Each pet will respond in an individual way to healing. When things have gone too far for improvement, healing offers the terminally ill pet a sense of peace in the last stages of life. If you wish, a professional healer can also give you healing at this time to help with the trauma of the situation. (See page 160 for information on healing for the terminally ill.)

GEMMA HAS A LONG LIFE

I was asked to give healing to Gemma, a black 19-year-old cat with a suspected liver tumour, to help her feel happy and peaceful in the last stages of her life. Her care-giver Joyce is someone that I've know for quite a while – she also has Santa the golden retriever dog who you can read about on page 184. Whenever I visited to give Santa his healing, Joyce brought Gemma to me lying on a large cushion. Although she looked very thin, Gemma had a strong spirit and really loved the healing, always purring loudly and stretching out her claws in ecstasy. Frequently she would get off the cushion to sit on the sofa next to me. Every month when I called, I wondered if Gemma would still be there. Joyce would open the door and say, 'Yes, Gemma's still with us,' and sure enough there she was snoozing on her cushion without a care in the world! We crossed our fingers as a whole year went by and Gemma was still holding her own and enjoying life. Nearly two years later, when Gemma was 21 years old, I got the very sad phone call to say that she had passed away. I remember Gemma with huge affection; she was a grand old lady and Joyce was thrilled that regular healing had helped during the last two years of Gemma's special companionship.

Healers come in all shapes and sizes

Healers are human beings and come in all shapes, sizes and ages, from a wide variety of backgrounds and with differing personalities. Most healers adopt a non-denominational approach to their work, recognising that everyone has their own beliefs and opinions. Animals, of course, do not have any concepts of faith, doctrine or religion, or of labels and descriptions. It is important that the healer you use for your pet is a person that you trust and have a rapport with, and is someone that you feel at ease with. If there is a personality clash then you will be tense while the healing is taking place. Your pet will pick up on that and the atmosphere will not be conducive to effective healing. There are healers out there to suit everyone and, as with all therapies, some healers have greater ability in their field than others.

Healer training

Training to become a member of a recognised professional organisation takes time and first of all the healer has to take courses which include working with humans. Some people say they just want to work with

animals, but all pets are involved with humans in some way, so healers need to be experienced with dealing with people before they specialise. The courses leading to full membership run by the UK's leading and largest healing organisation, the NFSH (National Federation of Spiritual Healers), last a minimum of two years. There is also now an NFSH link in the USA offering healer training. There are several modules in their training programme, which cover topics such as the holistic and spiritual nature of healing, the physical body, the invisible bodies, energy centres, understanding the nature of disease, meditation and visualisation, stress management and of course practice in giving healing and sending out distant healing. During the training period, tutors offer mentor support and healing supervision at regular group meetings. The NFSH is a non-denominational organisation and respects the right of every individual to hold his or her own interpretation of the source of healing energy.

'With hands of love and light, the healer is the earthly connection for the cosmic source of healing energy.'

All members of the NFSH take the same syllabus to the same standard. They are permitted to give healing within the National Health Service on a doctor's referral. Many healthcare workers, including doctors and nurses, as well as numerous practitioners in complementary therapies, both human and animal, have taken healer training. Some healers may even go on to specialise in certain areas, such as cancer patients or the terminally ill, for example. Other healers such as myself devote themselves to working with animals. The NFSH has also recognised the need for a register of animal healers and I am delighted to be teaching both their equine and small animal healing courses. These are open to healer members after they have completed their initial training and who have the relevant animal experience.

There are other skills that are essential in order to be an effective professional healer. Empathy and enthusiasm are vital attributes as this means the client will enjoy the time spent with the healer, and be more relaxed. It goes without saying that a healer specialising in animals must be passionate about them and their well-being. People who seek out healers are frequently upset or worried about themselves, someone else or their pet, so good counselling skills and a sympathetic listening ear are vital. I advise all my healer students to take a counselling course at a local college and also a course in anatomy. All knowledge gained is helpful, and even though healers do not make a diagnosis or prescribe anything, understanding the nature of a problem means that they are able to offer stronger emotional support. It is difficult to remain detached when dealing with another's problems, but that is something that the healer must do to guard against becoming too involved and therefore too

drained. This is something I personally find hard, particularly with an animal that I have been helping for a period of time. I have to admit to getting quite fond of my furry and feathery clients!

Fees

Registered healers usually make a charge for their time and expenses, including distant healing, and there are also other outgoings, such as office expenses, professional fees and further training that they have to cover. There are no set fees and these will vary, depending on whether the healer has to pay rent for their premises, the type of clinic they practise from and other considerations.

How the healer will work

When you contact the healer, ask them to explain what their experience with animals is and what types they have given healing to. Some healers, for example, work better with certain species of animals and may have a speciality or preference. Each healer will have their own way of working, but the principles will be the same in that they will lay their hands on, or just above, the body of the pet. All individual healers develop a technique that works best for them. With distant healing, some healers just ask for the pet's name, while others will request a photograph to be sent to help them focus on sending out the healing.

How many healing treatments will the healer give?

The number of treatments needed will depend on the condition being treated, the age of the animal, and its response to the healing. Chronic conditions will usually need more sessions than acute ones. In my experience if the problem is purely emotion-based, then one or two treatments are generally enough, provided there are no other considerations. For therapeutic healing when the animal is healthy, a session every three to six months is, I find, normally adequate. Obviously this is based on my own experience and healers vary in their individual approach.

12 Other natural therapies

When one person has a dream alone, it remains a dream. When many people have a dream together it is the beginning of a new reality.

Hundertwasser

Our pets are very complex creatures and, as many things can go wrong, it is absolutely essential that a vet is consulted for an initial diagnosis for any concerns. This should include changes in behaviour as these can indicate pain, distress or illness. *It is important that we never attempt to guess what is wrong and treat our pets ourselves, or try complementary therapies at home first rather than take the animal to a vet. The animal can suffer as a result.* The vet can refer your pet to other members of the therapeutic team as required. Through good communication with all the specialist animal healthcare practitioners the pet can receive the broadest range of suitable treatments.

As explained earlier in the book, healing can sometimes set up a process of recovery that may stimulate enough improvements without other natural therapies being involved. However, I am a great believer in the holistic team approach as it is very beneficial – and in many cases, essential. Other therapies all work at their individual levels to promote better health and improved well-being for our pets. These therapies may treat individual symptoms or work to influence changes on many levels. All will affect the energy field of the animal in some way.

Healing can be used alongside any other treatment, not least because illness, pain and discomfort are very stressful for any animal and healing offers peace. Most importantly, and something that I have come across many times as a healer, if the pet is harbouring feelings of grief, resentment or anger, then these feelings may prevent other therapies from working as effectively, or as deeply, as possible. Healing can help the animal to 'let go', which can release tension before other therapies are applied. If one area of the animal's body is disturbed it will have a knock-on effect somewhere else – *everything* needs to be in balance.

Healing works in the energy field affecting all the levels at once, and aims to establish homeostasis (which means balance). The way I see it is

that healing provides a foundation for the other therapies to work in synergy with the body and each other, because otherwise the therapies are working with chaotic energy. In my experience this means that the treatments may be more effective, can work at the deepest possible level and fewer sessions or remedies may be required.

Sometimes therapies produce what's known as a 'healing crisis', which means that for a short time things can temporarily get worse before they get better. However, this doesn't happen with healing by laying on the hands. An animal may be sleepy for a while after healing or it may even be energised, but there will be no negative results. This is not to say that there is going to be a cure or that you will get the improvements or changes that you particularly want. Changes or adjustments will take place on whatever level is possible.

Healing aims to produce balanced and harmonious energy and other therapies can make good use of that energy. There are many therapies that healing works well alongside and I have listed below the ones of which I have personal experience. In each section I explain how healing helps alongside these therapies.

Musculo-skeletal problems

Like humans, animals can suffer from neck and back ache, headaches, aching joints, muscle problems, acute pain, inflammation, shooting pains and general stiffness. Problems can be caused by many factors – slips, falls, road traffic accidents, injuries, general surgery, tension and old age. Sometimes trauma goes undetected and the poor function of the spine increases the effort in other areas until the animal cannot function properly generally and starts limping or goes lame. Dogs that pull persistently against a collar or harness, and guide dogs that constantly walk on one side of their handler, often have musculo-skeletal problems. Working and competition dogs frequently suffer from injuries to legs and backs. Their performance and general well-being can be helped by having regular preventative and maintenance treatments.

Natural therapies can help to improve an animal's quality of life and your vet can advise you on the one most suitable for your pet.

Acupuncture

Acupuncture is mostly practised on dogs, cats and horses, but other animals can also benefit. Other species that respond to acupuncture include cattle, pigs, parrots, birds of prey, rabbits, guinea pigs and rats. Pets can benefit from acupuncture for a wide range of conditions including joint problems, pain and inflammation, muscle spasms, wound repair, lameness, nerve problems, and after accidents. Acupuncture can be given to induce labour and to help animals during the process of giving birth. Incontinence can be very much helped in female dogs and cats and some inflammatory skin problems in domestic pets can also respond to acupuncture. Acupuncture can be given to horses to improve endurance and stamina.

During a treatment very fine needles are used over specific points, but for sensitive or worried pets a special laser, photonic or electrical stimulation pen can be used instead. When the needle reaches a specific point there can be a sensation like a dull ache and some pets may find this uncomfortable on occasion. The pen is gentler and less invasive so does not produce this discomfort. Of course, some animals just do not like having needles stuck into them so this can be a good option. Sometimes I've given healing before acupuncture was administered to help open up the meridians. In some very acute cases, I've given healing while the vet was applying the acupuncture.

The classical Chinese explanation of acupuncture is that there are energy highways (meridians or channels) running in regular patterns through the body and over its surface. Meridians are where electricity flows in a low resistance. The needles stimulate specific points along the meridians, triggering the release of chemicals, hormones and nerve impulses that influence the animal's internal regulating system. During a healing treatment I can often feel with my hands where there are blockages in the meridians and also the energy changes. The more healing that you practise, the more sensitive you will become to picking up these sensations. Hands-on healing is compatible with acupuncture as both are balancing therapies and both work with the bio-electric movement of the body to promote a natural return to better health.

Note: *In the UK, it is the law that only a veterinary surgeon may administer acupuncture to an animal.*

Physiotherapy

It is important to know who is properly trained in physiotherapy with qualifications that your vet will recognise. In the UK look for the title 'chartered physiotherapist'. These practitioners have undergone extensive full-time training to degree level before taking a post-graduate course in

animal or veterinary physiotherapy. In the USA the letters PT after a name is an indication of professional training. Animal physiotherapists specialise in treating the musculo-skeletal system of a wide range of species, including dogs, cats, chickens, ducks, goats, rabbits, sheep, horses, farm animals and zoo animals.

Many of today's animal physiotherapists have extended their knowledge into the field of energy medicine, recognising that the body will respond to subtle stimuli such as cranio-sacral therapy or other gentle energy techniques. Cranio-sacral therapy is also often practised by osteopaths and chiropractors. It is a very gentle body rebalancing treatment through special hand techniques on the cranium (skull), spine and sacrum (hip area).

Depending on the particular problem, physiotherapists may also use special laser or electro-therapy equipment. Physiotherapy works mechanically within the energy field that runs through the muscles, ligaments, tendons and bones of the animal, and therefore healing can prepare or help to maintain strong energy flow in these areas, and also stimulate soft tissue repair.

We have found in our clinic that sometimes the physiotherapists cannot treat the animal because there is a deep emotional problem. In these cases, I have been asked to give healing first to rebalance the animal, allow it to express and release emotional blockages and discharge the negative energy. Afterwards the physiotherapists have noticed a beneficial change to the function of the physical body and have been able make the necessary adjustments.

Chiropractic

Chiropractic is suitable for all animals and is a gentle holistic manipulation therapy. Like osteopaths, animal chiropractors first qualify to treat humans before specialising, unless they are already trained as vets. Practitioners use the hand to assess and treat all the bones of the spine and limbs. The chiropractor will check the whole of the skeleton to discover any subtle misalignments of the bones. These misalignments can impinge on nerve pathways feeding from the spine and affect the animal's muscles, joints and major organs. This can damage the animal's overall health as well. A direct thrust is applied by the hand on a specific part of the bone involved. This causes a reflex action which allows surrounding ligamentation to instantly relax and then contract. This lets the body's innate healing process encourage alignment. Conditions that can benefit from chiropractic are the same as for osteopathy.

180

Osteopathy

Osteopathy is a discipline involving the diagnosis of structural problems in humans and animals. Attention is generally, although by no means always, directed to the spine. In the UK the osteopath's full-time training over four years leads to a BSc degree and then practitioners can take a further post-graduate course of study in animal osteopathy. Osteopathic treatment involves making subtle and gentle adjustments to bones, muscles, tendons and ligaments. Cranio-sacral therapy is also used. The pets most commonly treated by osteopaths are cats and dogs who have suffered from trauma to the spine, head and pelvis. There are osteopaths who specialise in treating exotic animals, such as those found in zoos, as well as those who treat farm animals and horses.

I have on many occasions given healing to animals who were receiving osteopathy treatments and healing has helped tremendously. On these occasions the combination of healing and osteopathy has resulted in some extraordinarily deep and positive changes.

Homeopathy

Like healing, homeopathy is a therapy that treats the whole body, not just the symptoms. Homeopaths and healers recognise subtle energies in the living body, which homeopaths call the 'vital force'. The vital force runs through the body and is responsible for its healthy function and defence against disease. Homeopathy relies on the energy of the individual remedy to work with the animal's vital force, whereas healers work in general terms with the universal energy field connecting to the animal.

Homeopathic vets take a case history to establish what type of personality the pet is so that the most suitable remedy and dose may be prescribed. This is called a constitutional remedy. Specific remedies and herbs can also be offered, depending on the problem, and potencies are chosen which are going to be the most effective.

By working alongside homeopathic vets, I have found that their remedies can be more effective in some cases when used with sessions of healing. The healing calms and clears away any blockages to allow the homeopathic remedies to go in deeper. With this combination, we've had beneficial results with a range of problems, including epilepsy, cancer, grief, shock, despression, kidney and liver disease, poor immune system and behavioural problems. Homeopathy is a very potent form of medicine and one of the major benefits is that it does not have the side-effects associated with conventional drugs and so does not poison the

body. Homeopathic vets tell me that they trained in this form of medicine because it enabled them to treat the actual source of the problem, rather than the symptom. Furthermore the animal's body is not flooded with unnatural substances that could cause other health problems.

Note: *In the UK only a veterinary surgeon may legally prescribe home-opathic remedies, herbs, flower essences and essential oils for an animal.*

BLOSSOM

Puppies and young dogs are usually fun to give healing to because of their lively interest in things going on around them. Although Blossom was only just 18 months old, she didn't act like a young dog. She lay on the table in our clinic looking subdued and depressed. Blossom had been very poorly for ten weeks with severe attacks of haemorrhaging diarrhoea and was also unable to eat normal food. Over the weeks, there had been numerous trips to the vets, including three weeks in intensive care being given blood transfusions and lots of medication. The dog had also been to a top veterinary centre for numerous tests that showed that she had a very low red blood cell count. Blossom was now being given weekly iron injections and was taking antibiotics. It was not surprising that she looked so very unhappy and dispirited, with a very poor coat and dull eyes.

As soon as I lay my hand onto Blossom, I picked up intuitively that there had been a blow to the head and all her body energy rhythms were very out of balance. Julie, who had brought her to me, confirmed that when she was five months old she had been kicked in the head by a horse, which had fractured her skull. I then noticed a large lump on her forehead. I gave Blossom healing to rebalance her generally so that her body could begin to help itself more. A bouncy, bright-eyed Blossom returned a week later and Julie told me that after the healing treatment she 'just seemed to come together' and turned into a normal dog again, all signs of illness gone. Julie had also taken Blossom to an orthopaedic vet/animal osteopath team and the vet diagnosed that he thought the current problems were related to the previous head injury. Blossom was subsequently treated by the osteopath and as a result the lump on her head had reduced in size considerably.

On her second visit to me, Blossom behaved how I would expect a young dog to behave. She was full of energy and fun, and during the healing session she wanted to play and nibbled my fingers throughout, a big change from the very lethargic dog that had come in the week before. Blossom never looked back and is now a very fit, boisterous and healthy three-year-old.

Conclusion

Learning is finding out what you already know,
Doing is demonstrating that you know it,
Teaching is reminding others that they know just as well as you
You are all learners, doers, teachers.

From *Illusions* by Richard Bach

Healing is an individual experience, yet it forms a partnership with our pets like nothing else can. It is a partnership of joining together on the deepest level of love, where mind, body and soul of both healer and receiver become one. Healing is surprisingly easy to give once the decision is taken to 'have a go'. Animals already know what it is and where it comes from, for they are great healers themselves. There is no animal that I have ever come across that has not been open to healing. In their kinship with us, animals have a power and a wisdom that we are in need of to fulfil our destiny; and of course they have a great deal to offer to enhance our lives in an everyday sense too. Once made, the connection of healing energy is eternal and forms the strongest bond possible, animal to human.

After my first book *Healing for Horses* was published I wondered what people would make of it. I have been rewarded immensely by receiving hundreds of letters from people who have found that the book has inspired them and changed their lives, because the healing opened up a whole new world. It confirmed what many people suspected already and gave them the confidence to know that not only could they be healers, but they could also communicate with their animals mind-to-mind and soul-to-soul. Following the guidelines in the book, these people have given healing to their horses and been amazed at the results, and how much it has opened up their communication.

My aim in this book is to help you discover the same inspiration with your pets – hands-on healing is for all of us, not just an elite few. Healing is so very rewarding and the feeling it brings as we connect with our pets is immense in its power. It is a feeling of oneness – with our inner being, our pet and the great universal source of all life.

Through giving healing to animals, I have come as close as is possible on earth to the sensation of being in paradise, of being acquainted with all knowledge, and feeling the great peace of being enveloped in the warmth of pure love. Animals give us this opportunity if we want to take it and healing is the key. I hope that you too will experience all these wonderful things as you embark on your journey as a healer with your beloved pets.

An Animal's Love

I came into your life
because I love you.

My love asks no questions of your past
or where you come from.
I see only your soul
and wish to heal you
for your future in eternity.

Choose to heal me too
with your loving touch.
We have only the present
to do this together,
so reach out and know my soul.

Margrit Coates

References and suggested further reading

Spiritual Healing: a practical guide to hands-on healing
Jack Angelo
Barrons
ISBN 0 7641 2159 6

Bach Flower Remedies for Animals
Stefan Ball & Judy Howard
C.W Daniel & CO
ISBN 0 85207 296 1

Communicating with Animals – the spiritual connection between people and animals
Arthur Myers
Contemporary Books
ISBN 0 8092 3149 2

Crystal Healing for Animals
Martin Scott and Gail Mariani
Findhorn Press
ISBN 1 899171 24 X

Healing Research: Volume 1 Spiritual Healing: validation of a healing revolution
Daniel J. Benor MD
Vision Publications
ISBN 1 886785 11 2

Healing Research: Volume 1 Professional supplement to Spiritual healing
Daniel J. Benor MD
Vision Publications
ISBN 1 886785 12 0

Kindred Spirits
Allen. M Schoen DVM
Souvenier Press Ltd
ISBN 0285 636502
and Broadway Books
ISBN 076790 4311

Natural Healthcare for Pets
Richard Allport MRCVS
Element Books
ISBN 0 00 713087 2

New Colour Healing
Lilian Verner-Bonds
Vermilion
ISBN 0 09 188386 5

Vibrational Medicine
Richard Gerber MD
Bear and Company
ISBN 1 879181 58 4

Wild Health
Cindy Engel
Weidenfeld & Nicolson
ISBN 0 297 64684 2

Author's acknowledgements

I have to start by thanking every animal I have met through whose eyes I have seen the soul energy – sometimes sad, sometimes fearful but thankfully often happy. All the creatures of the world are my healing teachers and prove to me the existence of a powerful and divine source of energy.

All of the people with whom I come into contact – including clients, colleagues, students, associates, friends and family – have in their own way contributed to this book through my experience of having known them. Every one has added something to my life and my knowledge and this process is ever ongoing.

I am indebted to my colleagues, homeopathic veterinarian Cheryl Sears for her invaluable professional advice and checking relevant sections of the manuscript, and veterinary physiotherapist Amanda Sutton for continuing to inspire me. My gratitude also to holistic vet Nick Thompson for his input and to pet behaviour therapist Jo Scott, who also advised me.

The photographs in this book are by Jon Banfield who, being married to a vet, is well aware that animals are difficult subjects to work with, but as always he has produced some great shots for me. It was a joy for me to work with the animal models for this book: Shona, Jakie, Mischief, Scrumpy, Bob, Dennis and Lily Kit. The illustrations are by colour pencil artist Bob Ebdon and I wish to thank him for creating such inspired pieces of work. Again I have been continually supported on this project by my publisher Judith Kendra and editor Sue Lascelles, plus all of the great team at Random House worldwide.

Finally, where would I be without my three cats Mitzi, Teddy and Lilly, who made me take frequent play breaks from slogging away on the manuscript of this book.

Useful addresses

The names and addresses listed here are given for information only and they do not imply any endorsement of the methods or opinions described in this book.

Animal healing

The Margrit Coates Foundation for
Animal Healing
PO Box No 1826
Salisbury
Wiltshire SP5 2BH
UK
website: www.theanimalhealer.com
*(Consultations by veterinary
referral only. Also write to Margrit
Coates for information on music for
animal healing. A stamped
addressed envelope would be
appreciated.)*

New World Music
The Barn
Becks Green
St. Andrews
Beccles
Suffolk NR34 8NB
tel +44(0) 1986 781645
tel for USA 1 800 771 0987
www.newworldmusic.com
*(Music for Animal Healing and
relaxation.)*

College of Psychic Studies
16 Queensberry Place
London SW7 2EB
tel 020 7589 3292
www.psychic-studies.org.uk
*(Healer training including for
animals.)*

National Federation of Spiritual
Healers (NFSH)
Old Manor Farm Studio
Church Street
Sunbury on Thames
Middlesex TW16 6RG
UK
Tel: 01932 783164
e-mail: office@nfsh.org.uk
website: www.nfsh.org.uk
*(Healer referral service. Details on
courses to train as a healer and
animal healing courses.)*

National Federation of Spiritual
Healers (NFSH) USA
315 Goldenwest Avenue
Ojai
California 93023
USA
Tel: 805 640 0211 or 805 407 5366
e-mail: Rogerford8@aol.com
(Various healing courses.)

Practitioners in other complementary areas

British Holistic Veterinary Medicine
Association (BHVMA)
The Secretary
Straid Veterinary Hospital
121 Station Road
Beaconsfield
Buckinghamshire HP9 1LH
UK
Fax: 01494 677333

American Holistic Veterinary
Medical Association
2218 Old Emmorton Road
Bel Air
MD 21015
USA
Tel: 410-569-0795
Fax: 410-569-2346
e-mail: AHVMA@compuserve.com
*(Maintains a directory of members
for referral information.)*

British Association of Homeopathic
Veterinary Surgeons
Tel: 01367 718115
website: www.BAHVS.com
*(Information on vets with an
interest in homeopathy.)*

Association of British Veterinary
Acupuncturists
85 Earls Court Road
London W8 6EF
UK
Tel: 020 7937 8215
Fax: 020 7460 0020
*(Information about vets with an
interest in acupuncture.)*

General Osteopathic Council
Osteopathy House
176 Tower Bridge Road
London SE1 3LU
UK
Tel: 020 7357 6655
(Information on animal osteopaths.)

The Association of Chartered
Physiotherapists in Animal Therapy
(ACPAT)
The Secretary
Morland House
Salters Lane
Winchester
Hampshire SO22 5JP
UK

Tel: 01962 844390
Fax: 01962 863801
e-mail: acpat@clara.net
website: www.acpat.org
*(Details of qualified animal
physiotherapists.)*

McTimoney Chiropractic
Association
3 Oxford Court
St James Road
Brackley
Northamptonshire
UK
Tel: 01280 705050
Fax: 01280 700117
*(Holds a directory of animal
chiropractors.)*

Animal welfare organisations

Animaline
The Lodge
Broadhurst Manor
Horsted Keynes
Hayward Heath
West Sussex RH17 7BG
UK
Registered Charity No 1031342
Tel: 01342 810596
Fax: 01342 811213
*(Fighting for the peace and dignity
of all animals.)*

World Society for the Protection
of Animals
14th Floor
89 Albert Embankment
London SE1 7TP
UK
Tel: 020 7587 5000
Fax: 020 7793 0208
e-mail: wspa@wspa.org.uk
website: www.wspa.org.uk

*(Acts against cruelty, exposes animal
abuse and rescues animals in
distress. Eleven offices and more
than 400 member societies in over
90 countries worldwide.)*

PDSA
Priorslee
Whitechapel Way
Telford
Shropshire TF2 9PQ
UK
Registered Charity No 208217
Tel: 01952 290999
Fax: 01952 291035
e-mail: pr@pdsa.org.uk
website: www.pdsa.org.uk
*(45 PetAid hospitals and over 260
PetAid practices.)*

The Humane Society of the United
States
2100 L Street NW
Washington
DC 20037
USA
Tel: 202-452-1100
Fax: 202-778-6132
website: www.hsus.org

National Canine Defence League
17 Wakley Street
London EC1V 7RQ
UK
Tel: 020 7837 0006
Fax: 020 7833 2701
e-mail: info@ncdl.org.uk
website: www.ncdl.org.uk
*(Campaigns on dog welfare issues
and runs nationwide re-homing
centres.)*

Chilterns Dog Rescue Society
Hog Lane
Ashley Green
Chesham
Buckinghamshire HP5 3NX
UK
Tel: 01442 876009
Registered Charity No 257557
*(Founded in 1963, the Society has
rescued and re-homed over 14,000
unwanted and abandoned dogs.)*

Better British Breeders
Pro Dogs National Charity
Rocky Bank
4 New Road
Ditton
Kent ME20 6AD
UK
Tel: 01732 848499
*(Members follow ethical breeding
practices.)*

The Rabbit Charity
PO Box No 23698
London N8 0WS
UK
Tel: 020 8888 0001
website: www.bunny.org.uk
*(Dedicated to public awareness and
education on rabbit welfare. Also
offers an adoption and re-homing
service.)*

Cats Protection
17 Kings Road
Horsham
West Sussex RH13 5PN
UK
Tel: 01403 221919
Fax: 01403 218414
e-mail: cpl@cats.org.uk
website: www.cats.org.uk
*(Rescue and re-homing centres,
neutering vouchers and education
on pet welfare.)*

Index